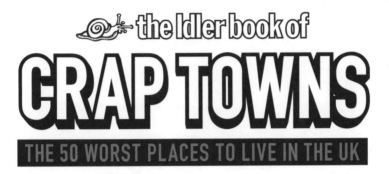

the Idler book of
CRAP TOWNS
THE 50 WORST PLACES TO LIVE IN THE UK

B🍃XTREE

First published 2003 by Boxtree an imprint of Pan Macmillan Ltd
Pan Macmillan, 20 New Wharf Road, London N1 9RR
Basingstoke and Oxford
Associated companies throughout the world
www.panmacmillan.com

ISBN 0 7255 1582 5

Extract from *Slough*, from *The Collected Poems* by John Betjeman,
reproduced with kind permission of John Murray (Publishers) Ltd
Extract from *Brave New World* by Aldous Huxley, first published in 1970,
reproduced with kind permission of Harper Collins Publishers Ltd
Extract from the *Selected Letters of Philip Larkin 1940-1985*,
reproduced with the kind permission of Faber and Faber Ltd

9 8 7 6 5 4

A CIP catalogue record for this book is available from the British Library

Typeset by Liz Harris
Printed by Bath Press

Edited by
Sam Jordison and Dan Kieran

Designed by Liz Harris

Illustrations by Gwyn

Acknowledgements and thanks:
Tom Hodgkinson, Gavin Pretor-Pinney, Matthew De Abaitua, Simon Benham,
Natalie Jerome, Eloise Millar, Rachel Poulton, Finlay Coutts-Britton,
Chris Jacob, Dan Gibbons, Dr Richard Miles, Paul Hamilton,
Chas Newkey-Burden, Daniel Etherington, Aaron Edwards, Angela Phillips,
Jon Fortgang, Sarah Janes, Kevin Parr, Henry Littlechild, Ben Hassett,
Jamie Dwelly, Matthew Clayton, Kevin Kieran, Gareth Kieran, Jill Kieran,
Diana Jordison, David Jordison, Anna Jordison, Amy Jordison, Liz Rowland,
Martin Casson, Mr Chittock, Susannah Herbert, Judy Munday, Roger Halton,
Rita Kieran, Michael Cumming, Ben and Nick Munday, Sarah Mc Cann,
Kieran Topping, Lawrence Pointer, Sue Plewes, Joe Lobley, Steve Chalk,
Sue Greenwood, Hugh Breton, Stephen Clarke, Pat Dennison, John Potter,
Colin Charde, Tom Espley, Ken MacKinnon, James White, Lisa Weatherley,
and 50 helpful council information services.

A NOTE ON STATISTICS:
GSCE RESULTS are based on the percentage of 15 year olds achieving five or more GCSE/GNVQ grades A–C from the results for 2002. The national average is 51.5. For Scottish towns, an equivalent is given based on Scottish Higher exam results.
CRIME: based on 'violence against the person' offences, April 2000 to March 2001.
POPULATION AND UNEMPLOYMENT FIGURES are based on the 2001 Census. Except where made up.

A NOTE ON THE RANKING SYSTEM:
This is based on the number of nominations each town received from the general public (before May 31 2003) which we then placed in ascending order. There was a bit of maths stuff involved in this, based on the population of each town. We weighted nominations from places with small populations so they stood more of a chance against the big cities. We didn't have to interfere too much though. We were always amazed by the number of people writing in about places we'd never heard of.

IT'S... THE... 1960'S TOWN PLANNERS!
GENTLEMEN. IF IT LOOKS LIKE A BUNKER, SMELLS LIKE A BUNKER AND ALLOWS SUNLIGHT IN LIKE A BUNKER: LOGIC DICTATES-THEN-THAT IT IS A LIBRARY, OR SCHOOL, HOSPITAL, OR TOWN HALL...
GWYN

BRITAIN IS CRAP. We can't lay any claim to the originality of the idea for this book. It was already out there, staring us in the face, snarling 'Whatchoo lookin' at' and lobbing beer bottles at us on a Friday night. It was ramming us in the back as we squeezed onto late trains, more crowded than cattle trucks. It charged us thousands of pounds in Council Tax and failed to clean up the mess right outside our front door. It told us we couldn't have fun, because it would lower the tone, and that we couldn't enter unless we had smart shoes and a collared shirt. It wasn't us that had the idea, it was the idea that had us – and then overcharged us for the privilege.

Our sole innovation was to use the internet to help spread the Crap Towns message. We wrote pieces about two towns we knew well, Morecambe and Alresford, put them up on the website of The Idler, and enquired if any of the magazine's readers had suffered similar experiences. The idea caught on fast.

Hundreds of Idlers wrote back to us, delighted at the opportunity to have a go at their unhappy homes. Soon word spread around chat rooms and web-logs and we quickly had far more nominations than our meagre work ethic could cope with.

Since then we have scoured the nation collecting nominations for Crap Towns until we could plot a Crap Map, each town denoted by a small brown pin. This map is filthy with grievances and all the various forms of misery the towns have inflicted, from inner-city poverty to self-satisfied middle England, from the dull and lifeless to the ugly and depressing, from concrete monstrosities to phoney heritage centres.

The fifty towns we've selected for this book are the places that have been nominated the most often by the public on the website and made us laugh the most. The entries are based on readers' emails, together with some contributions from friends of The Idler. We contacted local authorities and MPs in all the towns and have included defences from those who chose to reply.

And just for the record, the entries don't always reflect our personal opinions. We like Hull. We really do. We like the people. We like their spirit. We don't understand why so many of our writers hate it so much. Perhaps it's because it smells of death.

Sam Jordison and *Dan Kieran*

50 ST ALBANS
Where history meets today

Population: 128,982
Unemployment: 0.9%
Violent crimes: 3.2
(per 1,000 per annum)
% achieving 5+ GCSE
grades A-C: 99
Famous residents: **The bones of St Alban (early Christian martyr), Jacqueline du Pré (briefly), Stephen Hawking, a lot of people who used to be in Neighbours**

St Albans is described in The Rough Guide to Britain as 'one of the most appealing towns on the outskirts of London'. The official blurb boasts of its fine Roman mosaics and a beautiful cathedral. It apparently has good shopping facilities, high standards of education, low unemployment and excellent transport links. It's also home to the Campaign for Real Ale. But it's still been nominated as a Crap Town. Here's why.

Having lived in St Albans since 1975 I have witnessed many changes to this historical and frankly suffocating satellite town. We have no cinema and more importantly no hospital, courtesy of 52 years of Conservative local government. We do have lots of pubs though. You can either drink with nauseating Morris-dancing CAMRA members or with drunken, violent polo-shirt wearing Neanderthals and their vacuous harridans. You have to be careful if you're black or gay or look a bit weird, because the lace curtains will be twitching and we don't like strangers who talk funny.
EDWARD BAILEY

TEEN RAMPAGE
Squadrons of malevolent bankers in Porsches constantly choke the roads. Anyone over the age of twenty not wearing a designer-jeans-and-fluorescent-shirt combination is considered a dangerous revolutionary. The (catastrophically bored) teenagers, meanwhile, pave the streets with their prone bodies after attempting to drink themselves out of their middle-England hell. Wearing over-sized Slipknot T-shirts and spikes through their noses, they long to die. A perfectly reasonable reaction to life in St Albans.
SAMUEL DAVIDS

PHOTO: SAM JORDISON

HISTORY MEETING
TODAY IN ST ALBANS

49 HINCHLEY WOOD

Dum defluant amnes
(Until the rivers run dry)

Population: **5,000**
Unemployment: **2%**
Violent crimes: **11.5**
(per 1,000 per annum)
% achieving 5 or more GCSE grades
A–C: **66**
Famous residents: **Chris Tarrant and Kid Jensen live quite nearby**

Until recently, Hinchley Wood epitomised British suburbia: quite leafy, quite prosperous, quite boring. Then McDonald's tried to set up a restaurant in the place of a pub. The locals rose up, carried out a brilliant campaign and kept the burgers out. They've become the inspiration for residents' associations all over the world.

The epic narrative that is the history of Hinchley Wood began in the 1930s when a petrol station was built on an A3 sliproad. And the people, attracted by the smell of gasoline and tyres, came and built upon this place, so that the petrol station wouldn't feel too lonely.

Soon there were a few shops and even more houses. And a train station. There is, quite simply, nothing else.

While time moved on in its normative linear patterns elsewhere, this blighted suburban limbo still clings to the Spirit of 1934. If you ever see a film set in an emotionally repressed, curtain-twitching Home Service suburban wasteland, chances are that you're looking at Hinchley Wood. Hinchley Wood lives in a temporal aspic so dense that it would be no real surprise to see Stanley Baldwin doffing his bowler hat at the Post Office.

And here in Hinchley Wood, the moribund drones of late capitalism move hither and yon in what must be the epitome of desiccated commuter-belt suburbia. It sucks the life out of you, like a mock-Tudor vampire. Had even Falstaff, Louis Armstrong or Christopher Biggins ever visited Hinchley Wood they would have most certainly lost the will to live within ten minutes.

This is only a place to live in the sense that it connects you to somewhere else. It is not a proper place at all. So if you want to live inside a space of radical indeterminacy and non-being then Hinchley Wood is the place for you. It's one

ALL HINCHLEY WOOD PHOTOS: LIZ ROWLAND

of the few ways, other than watching reruns of Alan Titchmarsh's early Nineties daytime chat show, to experience the sensation of death while still – technically at least – alive and breathing.

Something interesting once happened in Hinchley Wood. Mikhail Gorbachev had dinner at the Hinchley Wood Berni Inn in 1995. It was somehow fitting that a man who lived the bathos of the broken dreams of World Communism should alight in dear old HW. Nowhere is more broken, or more bereft of vision, humanity or hope than HW.

Indeed, back in the Seventies, some desperate Hinchley Woodite had scrawled 'Abandon Hope All Ye Who Enter Here' on top of the steps leading from the train station. So apposite

CRAP TOWN TRIVIA McDonald's recently tried to build a restaurant in a Hinchley Wood pub. The residents waged a determined, brilliant campaign to keep them out. The tactics they used (including a picket of Downing Street) and their razor-sharp deconstruction of local planning-rules (proving how biased they are against locals and in favour of corporations) have become an inspiration to residents' associations all over the world. They may well help stop many of the abuses that make towns bad in the first place. Just goes to show that there's hope for Crap Towns everywhere. Or, how wrong we can be.

was this graffiti that it wasn't removed for over fifteen years.

GREG ROWLAND

....

IN DEFENCE OF HINCHLEY WOOD

Your correspondent has not looked beneath the surface of an area which at first sight is indeed unpromising. In my judgement, and experience, the people living in Hinchley Wood have a strong sense of community values and are prepared to stand up for them. The sense of community spirit, which rallied residents in Hinchley Wood to battle against McDonald's in recent years, has been evident in many ways. I saw it again recently in celebrating fifty years of St Christopher's Church –

one of the more impressive events of its kind I have seen in a local parish.

There is no doubt that the development of Hinchley Wood was due to eager property developers providing affordable new housing in the Green Belt attractive to the London commuter. Also, with Southern Railways' active promotion of their new electric train service, which was fast, clean and straight into the capital, it is not surprising that Hinchley Wood became, and still is, a popular place to live. What arrogance your correspondent has to dismiss 'suburbia' as if it were a no-go area.

Hinchley Wood may not have all the characteristics of 'chocolate box' Britain but it compensates with a cheerful character. Tourists may not have it on their map, but for those who live there the claim that it 'sucks the life out of you' is certainly not shown by the vibrancy of local activities to which I get invited.

IAN TAYLOR, MBE, MP

48 WIDNES

Industria ditat
(Hard work enriches)

Population: **53,000**
Famous residents:
Mel C (Sporty Spice)

It claims to be in Cheshire but was once in Lancashire yet should really be in Merseyside: which helps explain the horrible accent.

The Widnes–Runcorn Bridge, as seen in *Merseybeat*, is the last place on earth that its many suicide jumpers see. The place is constantly under the shadow of vapour clouds from the Fiddlers Ferry power station. The rain, when it mixes with all the chemicals in the air, must be the main reason why everybody looks like an extra from the film *Deliverance*.

Widnes, the place where the majority of the carcasses from the foot and mouth epidemic were incinerated.

SIMON BARKER

47 BARROW-IN-FURNESS

Semper Sersum (Ever forward)

Population: **60,000**
Unemployment: **4.1%**
Famous Residents: **Emlyn Hughes,
Legionella Pneumophila**

Isolated on a windswept peninsula on the southern extremities of Cumbria, Barrow is a ship-building town where hardly any ships are built, a shadow of its former self, dependent on the manufacture of a few murderous nuclear submarines for its survival.

Grey pebble-dash galore, Barrow is never without rain for more than a few minutes, and most people have only heard of it thanks to a well-publicised outbreak of Legionnaires Disease.

The near-redundant shipyard provides the glorious skyline of rusting cranes, beautifully set in front of the offshore rigs. The fish-stench-ridden indoor market has recently been threatened by Barrow's greatest achievement (bar the bowling alley) – Debenhams. The youth can now aspire to working in the department store, thus doubling their list of aims in life next to working in McDonald's.

Nightlife includes the club Martinis with its mock-marble interior and revolving dance

floor – I challenge you to stay on your feet after midnight when the floor is covered in cheap vodka and vomit.

Barrow also provides a gateway to the small secluded island of Walney; visitors can marvel at the lashing rain and gale force winds direct from the Irish Sea. Walney's biggest boast is The Roundhouse Chinese Takeaway, made famous by the murder of its owner who was found in pieces outside the establishment. It does cracking special fried rice with minimal gristle.

CLAIRE HOWSON

 So prodigious was the alcohol intake of the residents of Barrow in the 19th century that it attracted the specific attention of several temperance movements. They set up missions in the gin-soaked town and did their best to convert the residents to the delights of tea drinking. Most of these zealots gave up in despair after a few years and emigrated to America.

Walney Island is the windiest lowland site in Britain.

46 SKELMERSDALE

Salus populi suprema lex
(The well being of the people is the supreme law)

Population: **37,100**
Unemployment: **7%**
Violent crimes: **0.37 (per 1,000 per annum)**
% achieving 5 or more GCSE grades A-C: **39.1**

Famous residents: **Richard Ashcroft, Sonia (briefly famous Stock, Aitken and Waterman protégé)**

Skelmersdale can trace its origins back to Roman times, but its current history really began in 1961 when it became the Northwest's first New Town. It was developed to provide housing and employment for struggling inner-city dwellers in Merseyside. At first it was quite successful with rapid population expansion. However, more recently Skelmersdale has become a victim of the problems it was built to alleviate.

GREEN UNPLEASANT LAND

In the Sixties, a concrete holding centre for Liverpool's working class was run up in the greenery of West Lancashire.

With the skill and cunning of a top matador, the government tempted around 40,000 Merseysiders to leave their homes and follow the promise of big firms and steady pay, clear air etc., only to see their jobs and prospects whisked away inside a decade. 40,000 people, many too poor to get a car, were trapped in a sinister concrete playground without so much as a rail

Skelmersdale Champion

Vol. 9 • Issue 14   3 April 2002

■ First pictures of controversial asylum seekers centre

'IT LOOKS LIKE A PRISON'

That's how council chief described proposed building shown below

link, hospital or county court.

I wanted to make a documentary about it for Granada, but John Carpenter bought the rights and remade it as Escape from New York.

In the rain, the place resembles an East German Butlins – grey, empty, with a lack of investment. The older ex-pat Scousers get a tear in their eye, now and then, when, carrying their shopping bags back to the grey identikit estates, they vaguely remember something before they moved here, something else ...

Postscript

Last year, the local council decided to spend thousands of pounds on several 'art installations' for the town's many roundabouts – no doubt for the benefit of visitors. The most prominent of these was a £25,000, 18-foot monolith. This, apart from its purple colour, was almost identical to the monolith in 2001: A Space Odyssey. Yes – in their eyes, we were monkeys, twatting

CRAP TOWN TRIVIA *A study of crime-rate trends in Merseyside found reduced crime when a group of Yogic Flyers was set up in nearby Skelmersdale. The crime rate reduced from the third highest in England and Wales to the lowest among metropolitan areas – according to the Natural Law Party.*

HAVE YOU FUCKING COMEDIANS QUITE FUCKING FINISHED? I'VE GOT TO LOCK UP!

GWYN

each other about the head with each other's bones. One young lad, in a brave act of defiance, grabbed an aerosol and gave 'em some instant art criticism. 'Crap', he scrawled on the side.

JOSH WHITE

....

IN DEFENCE OF SKELMERSDALE

The Skelmersdale described in the article is not the town that we recognise.

We suggest you travel around the town and see the impact that the millions of pounds of public and private sector investment have had in terms of improved residential areas; the creation of new jobs; provision of top-class leisure and community facilities and good town centre services including one of the country's most modern superstores.

By visiting the town you will realise:

• Skelmersdale is prosperous, optimistic and attractive. It has good public transport and excellent road links.

• The spurious comments made about the people of Skelmersdale are insulting and inaccurate. Also, there have never been any riots.

• The artworks on roundabouts – paid for by special Government funds, not Council cash – attract investment and improve the image of the town.

We also suggest that you talk to local residents, shopkeepers and to the editors of the local papers who have a strong interest in investigative journalism. That will enable you to gain an accurate, fair and balanced picture of Skelmersdale.

WEST LANCASHIRE DISTRICT COUNCIL STATEMENT

THE SKELMERSDALE MONOLITH.
LIKE THE ONE IN '2001:
A SPACE ODYSSEY', BUT CRAP.

45 YATE
Pride and perseverance

Population: 23,000
Unemployment: 1.4%
Violent crimes: 7.6
(per 1,000 per annum)
% achieving 5+ GCSE grades A-C: 37
Famous residents: Prince Charles lives not too far away, JK Rowling lives in nearby Chipping Sodbury. No one famous appears to actually live within the Yate boundaries though

Yate is a modern English town; ugly lumps of concrete clustering around a hideous shopping mall. The surrounding countryside and nearby Chipping Sodbury are remarkably beautiful – but don't let that persuade you to go there.

Extruding like a textbook hernia from the soft underbelly of Bristol, the vast 1960s proto-newtown of Yate once enjoyed a claim to being the suicide capital of Western Europe, until the inhabitants acquiesced to the local anaesthetic of a revamped Tesco and brand-new Lidl mart.

Yate shopping centre is rumoured to have bannered itself 'Yate is great', but is in truth a Stalinist concrete shopping lubyanka – a quadrant of cold alleys perfectly designed to trap and funnel the wind.

From the centre, endless ranks of Bovis-style homes radiate to the horizon over trolley-packed streams and along roads with names that don't even try to be interesting.

The closest this open-plan wasteland has come to being interesting is the recent committal by magistrates of Gary Glitter after service technicians at a nearby PC World discovered his penchant for paedophilia. Fortunately, the subsequent trial didn't draw a jury from Yate itself, where there is little else to do but yearn for the relative fascination of a life in the Orkneys. Twinned not, as one graffito once quipped, with Legoland, Yate's true alter ego is Bad Salzdetfurth, which is another post-industrial abomination somewhere near Hanover but which, within all reason, can't be as wrist-slittingly forlorn as this forgotten overspill.

SIMON HACKER

44 BRIDGWATER
The home of the carnival

Population: **35,900**
Unemployment: **4.3%**
Violent crimes: **8.6 (per 1,000 per annum)**
% achieving 5+ GCSE grades A-C: **33**
Famous residents: **Julien Temple lives nearby, as did the late Joe Stummer**

Bridgwater lies about fifty miles southwest of Bristol, conveniently close to the M5. The River Parrett runs through the town from the Bristol Channel and on to Taunton. Once the river provided a vital industrial link deep inside the Southwest. This was until the inhabitants of Bridgwater built a bridge across the river, forcing the tall ships to stop there, and beginning their illustrious history as a port. A history which has all but ended.

BRIDGE OVER TROUBLED WATER

Like some kind of Wild West ghost-town, it has remained a dusty, hollow shell, trading on days of past glories.

Huge main roads, lined with railings, criss-cross Bridgwater. Old, badly built Victorian houses gently crumble away while modern monstrosities stand awkwardly next to them, just waiting for their ultimate decay. The dust, dirt and exhaust fumes conspire together in an attempt to kill what may be left alive which hasn't been run over.

Bridgwater has a carnival once a year. Interesting you might think. But, as with most things in Bridgwater, it's crap. Rather than have it during the summer when it's nice and warm and may attract lots of tourists, it is held in November when cold winds blow straight up from the Bristol Channel. I think the only reason they hold it is to give them something better to do than commit suicide.

ROB WESTLAKE

....

IDLER ROVING REPORTER'S VERDICT

I arrived at three in the afternoon, anxious to be fair to this noble Saxon town. I walked the length of the high street, trying to ignore the strange smell in the air, and was staggered when I saw the state of the black river/open sewer. Needless to say I left sharpish, fearful that tentacles of the black depression that seemed to afflict the inhabitants of this place would envelop me.

DAN KIERAN

The Poet
SAMUEL TAYLOR COLERIDGE
preached in this Church
on Sunday 4ᵀᴴ June 1797
and Sunday 7ᵀᴴ January 1798

CRAP TOWN TRIVIA

...NOR ANY DROP TO DRINK

The visionary poet Coleridge lived near (not in) Bridgwater in the late eighteenth century. It seems that even then, it was a crap town. Of a visit to the local hustings, he writes: 'Pacing the boards [I] mused on Bribery, False Swearing, and other foibles of Election Times.' Later he wanders down to the dock to look at the merchant ships, and writes of the water being 'as filthy as if all the Parrots in the House of Commons had been washing their consciences therein'.

A TOURIST OFFICER'S WORK IS NEVER DONE

BILGEWATER

The smell your reporter noticed is the local cellophane factory; it stinks worse than a week-dead skunk. But other than Fads and Halfords it's about the only employer in town, that is if you discount tar shops and feather stores. Indeed, the goodly, slack-jawed gawpers we laughingly call the inhabitants seem undeterred by the acrid air or recent dis-

BRIDGWATER NOT CRAP SAYS PUNK HERO

Idler editor
Tom Hodgkinson writes

Shortly before he died, I met Joe Strummer at the house of a mutual friend. Having just read the Crap Towns entry for Bridgwater, and knowing that the great man himself lived near that dark town, I thought I would try to endear myself to him by laughing about how crap Bridgwater was. I was also

closures that Bilgewater has a lower average IQ than anywhere else in Somerset.

Something to do with the acrid smell perhaps? This is a truly scary thought.

ROB WESTLAKE

....

IN DEFENCE OF BRIDGWATER

Bridgwater is a small busy town which is friendly and unpretentious. In terms of location, Bridgwater has it all.

Set at the foot of the Quantock Hills, it's a few miles from some of the best beaches in the Southwest and forty minutes from Bristol.

The town is also home to the largest illuminated carnival in Europe. Forget Notting Hill – this fabulous procession features over 120 entries, each one pulsating with music and aglow with the lights from thousands of coloured light bulbs, fantastically coloured costumes and special effects to create a magical evening of entertainment. Over 120,000 people attend the carnival each year visiting from all over the country and overseas.

NICK WHITE, SEDGEMOOR TOURISM UNIT

going to add how outrageous I thought it was that Bridgwater Council claimed Joe as a resident, when in fact he lived outside it.

'Bridgwater's not crap!' shot back the godfather of punk. 'It's a fantastic place. It's like Moss Side in the West Country.'

I instantly felt like a metropolitan scoffing snob. I couldn't think of any way of back-pedalling, as I had very definitely said Bridgwater was crap.

Then I remembered that this wasn't my personal view, but the view of the reader who nominated Bridgwater.

'Well, I didn't say it was crap, it was someone who lived there.'

'You'd better not tell Julien Temple you think it's crap. He'll be coming round and knocking on your door.'

Julien Temple is the well-known film director, and had just bought a house in Bridgwater. Joe went on to describe Bridgwater as a sort of outlaw town, hence its attraction for renegades such as himself and Julien Temple.

I felt at a loss for anything to say, so I was greatly relieved when Joe's wife Lucinda changed the subject by interjecting: 'Now Taunton? That really is a crap town.'

43 ALRESFORD

Population: 5,000
Famous residents:
John Arlott, the
Watercress railway
line (once visited by
Philip Schofield)

During the day gymkhana girls and rugby boys rule this rural backwater, but at night hundreds of bored Gangsta Rap enthusiasts congregate outside the chemist on the High Street and threaten passers by. It's purgatory with hanging baskets. As with most middle England enclaves, the only non-white residents work in Chinese and Indian restaurants. A few years ago the local council finally relented after pressure from the inhabitants and agreed to allow a fish and chip shop to open. The reason for their reluctance? 'It would lower the tone.'

Great if you're three or 53, shite if you're anywhere in between.

DAN KIERAN

PHOTO: DAN KIERAN

42 SLOUGH
Serve with honour

Population: 119,000
Unemployment: 3%
Violent crimes: 11.1
(per 1,000 per
annum)
% achieving 5 or
more GCSE grades A-C: 50.5
Famous residents:
Isambard Kingdom Brunel,
John Nash, William
Herschel, Faith Brown, Geri
Halliwell

'Come, friendly bombs and fall on Slough / It isn't fit for humans now,' blathered former Poet Laureate John Betjeman; in between attempting to rescue the Euston Arch and penning his banal odes. Never a more appropriate word was uttered though. JB was a bit of a fruitcake, but he knew a shit hole when he saw it and ever since he wrote his famous poem about the town, Slough has been a by-word for failed urban planning and concrete ugliness.

The only apparent reference to any culture is the name of Brunel on some of the municipal buildings, the design of which would no doubt leave the great engineer turning in his grave.

I end up in Slough quite a lot on business. There's no other reason to visit the depressing pit. Strung out along the old A4 (possibly in an attempt to rob rich nobs on their way from London to Windsor), it seemingly takes an age to drive through (or is that just time slowing down?).

The fields around Windsor Castle are probably only two miles away but to all intents and purposes it seems like an eternity …

DAN JOHNSON

WORTH PRESERVING?
Betjeman, whose first verse continues 'There isn't grass to graze a cow', would today have to eat his words. Between Upton Park, Langley Park, Black Park, Salt Hill Park and numerous open fields, there certainly is room to graze several cows. Or horses.

There was a publication of a book of poems written ages ago by local inhabitants to 'answer' Betjeman's famous contribution to Slough's reputation. It was terrible. I looked at it once – a paperback book (very thin). Then I put it back on the shelf and haven't seen it since. Similarly, in 1998, Slough Council encouraged people to defend the town against Betjeman. Ben Okri entered. I've been told News Room

University

Southeast did a piece on it, in which he stated that the fact that he'd never been to the town or driven past it did not prevent him from writing about it.

There are the down-points to Slough. For example, the dog turds on the pavements, the concrete lump that passes as a bus station, the unpleasant

CRAP TOWN TRIVIA

The popular comedy series The Office is based in Slough. The borough council asked star Ricky Gervais to become a cultural ambassador for their town after he rubbished it in the programme. He refused.

Gerry Anderson used to film Thunderbirds in an industrial unit on the Trading Estate but can no longer remember which one.

CAITRIONA LAWRENCE

31

smell of the municipal carparks. However, I would like to point out that there is currently a planning application to knock down the Brunel Bus Station along with plans to redesign the road layout through the centre of Slough. So things are not as bad as they are painted and they are going to improve still further.

CAT

SICKLY SWEET

A friend brought to my attention that Slough is noted in a canal-users' guide as being 'dull and uninteresting' and I do believe it is the general consensus.

I chose to relocate from the wonderful maritime city of Liverpool to the unfriendly, anonymous Slough – why? Temporary insanity is my only alibi.

I find myself drifting into a somewhat uncertain slumber every evening to the familiar noises of crashes on the M4 and planes landing at Heathrow – wondering if the next 747 will misjudge its landing and enter my bedroom.

Slough has been the home of Mars Bars since they were first made there in 1932 (the only sweetness in the place). There's bugger all else. In the summer it smells like crap, a mixture of exhaust fumes, airplane fuel and sewage works and the rest of the year is not dissimilar.

And yet people keep coming - more houses are being built upon once green pastures, immature offices are bulldozed for the new. Slough is an ever-expanding empire – where will it all end?

AMANDA SHELDRAKE

DESPONDENT WITH SLOUGH

A resident of Cookham Dean, marketing consultant Sam Sethi is campaigning for the SL postcode to be dropped from Windsor and Maidenhead and replaced with WM as residents no longer wish to be associated with Slough. In a survey carried out by Mr Sethi, 95% of respondents from Windsor and Maidenhead supported his cause.

Covering Marlow, Bourne End, Wooburn, Bray, Cookham, Burnham, Taplow, Dorney and Cippenham

MAIDENHEAD ADVERTISER

25p

Advertising: 01628 680680

Berkshire's biggest selling paid-for weekly newspaper

FRIDAY, JANUARY 17, 2003

Showgirls
Jubilee musical magic at St Marks

Tuck in
Sunday lunch for the family to be won

What's On
Hamlet gets a radical overhaul

GET MOTORING: 20 pages of new and used cars STARTS P73

Slough postcode is 'bad for borough'

Insurance up and prestige down, says

Police hail success of replica gun amnesty

INSIDE
Teen killers jailed

41 DAGENHAM
Judge us by our deeds

**Population: 155,000
(including Barking)
Unemployment: 4%
Violent crimes: 23.1
(per 1,000 per
annum)**
% achieving 5 or more
GCSE grades A-C: 42
Famous residents: Max
Bygraves, Jimmy Greaves,
Alf Ramsey, Sandie Shaw

Barking and Dagenham is a
borough of London, but is usually associated with Essex – more
specifically, the Essex that has
become the butt of the rest of the
nation's jokes. The huge car factories that used to dominate life
here are disappearing. The once
thriving industrial landscape has
become a barren wasteland of
empty warehouse shells and
stony rubbish. It's ugly.

ALL DAGENHAM PHOTOS: DAN KIERAN

One of those seething, white suburbs where everyone seems to be utterly, utterly furious for much of the time.

Hieronymus Bosch did most of his paintings in Dagenham. The inhabitants of Dagenham are the ugliest people in the world. It struck me, during the desperately unhappy teenage years that I spent there, that 70 per cent of the population appeared to bear appalling industrial injuries, including children and babes-in-arms. I remember once, while on a vacation from university, feeling conspicuous and vulnerable in the glittering high street. So I affected a limp and suddenly I seemed to blend in.

It's two-up, two-down terrace boxes for about 100 square miles. Its low-lying flatness ensures that a constant chilling wind circulates the carcinogenic flatulence that belches from the Thameside factories.

Dagenham has no need of a bookshop.

I haven't been back since 1992. In 2001 Dagenham's main employer, Ford, announced the closure of its factories there. I bet it's even nicer now.

PAUL SPRATLEY

40 KEIGHLEY
By worth

Population: **60,000**
Famous residents: **The person who invented the term 'Angel Delight'**

Martin Newell immortalised the place when he wrote: 'I'll tell you once and I'll tell you briefly, I don't want to go to Keighley.'

Given the option, I'd have not gone there either, but you can't help where you're born.

VICTORIA BARLOW

39 HASTINGS
Popular with visitors since 1066

Population: **85,000**
Unemployment: **4%**
Violent crimes:
22.7 (per 1,000 per annum)
% achieving 5 or more GCSE grades A-C: **35**
Famous residents: **Paula Yates, 'Mad' Penny from Big Brother**

Hastings is one of the many faded Victorian seaside resorts that line the English Channel – with the added historical attraction of an ancient castle and the battle that happened in its vicinity. Thanks to its current poor reputation, it also offers some of the cheapest housing available in Southeast England. A lot of good work is being done to transform Hastings, and soon it may be a fine place to live. Not yet though.

Hastings is a town that the rest of the South of England forgot. No roads go there (look at a road atlas). Walking along the seafront is like walking into a very bad version of the 1960s – but with less money about. Fashion left the town in 1959, and the finest public buildings are two public lavs – one on the seafront, one in the town centre.

The main tourist attraction is the castle – there's a delightful path leading from here to the seafront, where tourists can often make out spotty teenagers humping each other, or admire the fine collections of needles left by junkies.

GWYN

In the summer, it's just about bearable – the thousands of language students who spend two weeks wondering why their parents have sent them to live in a hovel really brighten up the place. In winter it's bleak, bleak, bleak – driving rain, sea winds and people smoking fags around Iceland (the closest Hastings gets to a deli).

The really sad thing about it is that everything around it is so fine – beautiful countryside, country villages, and a town that time forgot …

IAN TESTER

Hastings has the second highest divorce rate in the UK.

IN DEFENCE OF HASTINGS

Hastings isn't one of your usual, bland, boring seaside resorts: it's got real character. We have some problems but at least we're doing something about them. We've got the biggest beach-based fishing fleet in Europe; one of the highest concentrations of medieval houses in the country; a three-mile-long promenade with wonderful flower beds; fantastic parks; and much more. Anyway, if people are going to bitch and carp, I'm happy for them to go elsewhere.

KEVIN BOORMAN OF HASTINGS BOROUGH COUNCIL

Comedian Rod Hull was pronounced dead at the Conquest Hospital in Hastings in 1999. When watching Manchester United take on Inter Milan, Rod, 63, had climbed onto his roof to adjust his TV aerial. Unfortunately he fell off the ladder, through his greenhouse and onto a concrete floor. Sad, but then, Emu was fucking annoying.

38 HUNTINGDON
A special kind of place

Population: 45,000
Famous residents: John Major, Sid Owen

Huntingdon is full of congealed burger joints, cheap shoeshops selling plastic instruments of torture that make Chinese footbinding look like a harmless bit of fun, and fashion emporia brimming with anorexic-sized garments made out of the same material they put inside pre-packed supermarket meat to soak up ooze.

It is said that when East Germans get nostalgic for what life used to be like behind the Iron Curtain, they come to Blighty for a trip down memory lane. Well, their first stop should be Huntingdon.

LORNA HUGHES

PHOTO: LORNA HUGHES

37 MAGHULL

Population: **50,000**
Unemplyment: **6%**
Famous residents: **None**

This dormitory town seven miles outside Liverpool is a mean-spirited, characterless and deluded suburb which fancies itself as a cut above the rest of Merseyside. Queuing up outside B&Q on a Sunday morning is the closest it gets to culture.

Contains Ashworth, that institution full of psychos which is always in the news. Every Monday, they test the sirens, which wail mournfully at the start of another week in Maghull.

MATTHEW DE ABAITUA

36 READING
A Deo et Regina
(From God And The Queen)

Population:
143,124
Unemployment:
2.3%
% achieving 5 or more GCSE
grades A-C: **44.3**
Violent crimes: **10.8**
(per 1,000 per annum)
Famous residents:
Kate Winslet, Kenneth Brannagh, Oscar Wilde (briefly)

Reading, the prosperous Thames valley town a stone's throw from London, is home to two internationally renowned music festivals. And it's blander than Bran Flakes. Poets have been inspired to write about Reading, but only to say how ugly they find the place, and how much they dislike it.

Jerome K. Jerome highlighted Reading's failings in Three Men in a Boat as 'a carbuncle on the Thames'. The town is famous as the unwelcome home of Oscar Wilde. In The Ballad of Reading Gaol he speaks for everyone who has spent time there: 'In Reading gaol by Reading town there is a pit of shame.'

Until recently, the only entertainment for a boy or girl growing up in Reading was a set of benches outside Boots the Chemist. The place had a smattering of pubs, all populated by either violent rockers or even more violent men in yellow pullovers, white socks ('The Casuals') or, the leitmotif of all provincial towns, the teenage gothic. The nearest functioning cinema was in Bracknell, the only clothes shop was a C&A, and the one 'restaurant' a Wimpy.

Reading was but 30 minutes from London, yet it felt like a lifetime away. London has Soho and Mayfair; Reading defined itself with Smelly Alley - a fish market in the centre of town, and the Butt's Center – a 1970s concrete shopping complex designed to attract gluesniffers from throughout the world.

A statue of Queen Victoria has her back to the town, so much did she hate it. The other statue in the town is of a lion, but the sculptor designed the legs backwards then killed himself.

The people were oily, thuggish and believed in queues above all else. Staring was considered a crime. One story is of a teenager who stole a bag from the station, ran home with it, looked inside, discovered it contained a bomb and threw it into his own (well, his mother's anyway) garden and split before it blew. Only someone from Reading could steal a bomb and blow up their mother's garden.

Nevertheless, it was a paradise in those days compared to what it is now. Benefiting from millions of pounds of renovation and a massive economic boom, Reading looks more like Bilbao. But insurance salesmen, estate agents, foreign exchange students and mobile telephone engineers populate it. It may be shiny and new, but the whiff of boredom, wretchedness and despair reminds one of the rotten foundations.

EL TURK

CRAP TOWN TRIVIA *Almost all of the advertising and market research polls in the UK are carried out in Reading because it's so reliably average for the nation as a whole.*

BAD COUNCIL

The town has had pretensions of grandeur since the council dribbled its consent to the building of the intensely banal shrine to corporate blandness, The Oracle. This cathedral of Americanised shallowness has been situated right in the middle of a town which boasts the 'IDR', the worst excuse for a blocked artery road in the overcrowded and rapidly concreting south. Yet thousands come to sit in endless traffic jams, fighting their way through the lung-busting smog to punch their way through to the exact same shop that they just left.

And surely this development epitomises Reading, a place where you can pay more to get less. The faceless corporations who want maximum profit at the expense of style, class, innovation and risk have taken this soulless town to their own soulless chest cavities.

CHRIS GIBSON

IN DEFENCE OF READING

Reading's historic importance as the county town of Royal Berkshire is often overshadowed by the fact that most people know it as a major transport interchange and as an important commercial centre – indeed the capital of the Thames Valley economic region.

While it's true that many international companies have chosen Reading as their home, thanks to its unrivalled communications network, and that we have some of the finest high-tech business parks in the Southeast, the people of Reading also celebrate a history spanning the last 1400 years …

Reading is one of the UK's top ten retail destinations, and is the only place outside London's Oxford Street where you will find the country's top four department stores in one location – Debenhams, House of Fraser, John Lewis and Marks & Spencer.

The arrival of the stunning Oracle Shopping and Leisure Complex has brought nearly 100

"THE SCULPTOR DESIGNED THE LEGS BACKWARDS THEN KILLED HIMSELF."

CRAP TOWN TRIVIA

The lion is anatomically incorrect because it has four knees. The lion saved the park, however, because Reading Council wanted to build a dual carriageway right through the only bit of green space in the city. It turned out this lion is of some historical interest, and so now the dual carriageway goes around the park instead.
VICTORIA HILEY

new shops to Reading, to join the established areas of Broad Street, Friar Street and St Mary's Butts.

DAVID MILWARD, MEDIA AFFAIRS MANAGER, READING BOROUGH COUNCIL

LION PHOTO: VICTORIA HILEY

35 BILLINGHAM
Faith

Population: **35,000**
Famous residents: **Roy Chubby Brown lives nearby**

Billingham is a new town that sprung up around the ICI chemical works built in the 1930s. At the time, Aldous Huxley hailed Billingham as 'an ordered universe in a world of planless incoherence' (Preface to modern edition of Brave New World, which made us laugh, bitterly, having grown up there). With the demise of ICI, what remains is a 'patch-work of soulless estates' (to quote one local councillor).

Billingham has been repeatedly cited in consumer index surveys as the cheapest place in Britain to live. I'm not surprised, given the vast amount of pound shops to be found in the brutal grey concrete Stalinist architecture of the town centre. In the 1980s, this turned into a nocturnal skateboard park-cum-gluesniffers alley. By the mid 1990s, it was the place to score crack and heroin (highest incidence of heroin abuse outside Edinburgh).

Tragically, a recent report for the Local Education Authority found that there is one book for every ten households in Billingham.

ANDREW STEVENS

34 NEWPORT
Terra Marique (By land and sea)

Population: **150,000**
Famous residents: **Johnny Morris, Feeder**

Newport, South Wales.
It is crap.
Why?
Have you been there?
The beach is crap as well.
I've lived here so long I haven't even got the energy to slag it off properly.

LEO

33 SOUTH WOODHAM FERRERS
The Manor Of Champions

Population: 18,000
Unemployment: 2%
Violent crimes: 9.2 (per 1,000 per annum)
% achieving 5 or more GCSE grades A-C: 70

How does one begin with South Woodham Ferrers? Perched on the banks of the scenic River Crouch in deepest, darkest, highlights and gold-shoes Essex, it used to be a tiny village, with weather-boarded houses and the occasional train that passed through on its way to Bradwell nuclear power station. However, the 1970s saw radical plans to turn South Woodham into a 'Riverside Country Town' which was 'The Place To Be'. The death knell on any charm in the place was sounded. Expansion followed, and now it has been transformed into a dormitory-town Legoland, only

"IT REALLY DOES HAVE STREET NAMES BASED ON THE LORD OF THE RINGS"

without any of the fun rides.

Its nauseating red and yellow brick housing estates were completed mainly in the 1980s and early 1990s – hardly a time known for tastefulness. The centrepiece of South Woodham is in fact the Asda Clock Tower, where heathen residents go to worship the God of Groceries. I doubt there are any more miserable places on this earth to grow up than South Woodham. It's not poor, or underprivileged, or even rough – it's just utterly, utterly soulless. It really does have street names based on Lord of the Rings; almost all the residents disappear on the 7.32 to Liverpool Street daily and spend their weekends polishing their 4x4s.

South Woodham Ferrers Town Council call themselves The Lords of the Manor of Champions on their website. Says it all really.

KELSA SMITH

32 DOVER
Do ever good

Population: **30,000**
Famous residents: **PG Wodehouse**

Most people when thinking of Dover think it will be horrible because of the immigration problems. They are Daily Mail readers, and therefore wrong and stupid. Immigrants are the best thing that ever happened to Dover, balancing out the hordes of horrible 12-year-old mothers, fat till-workers called Stacey and skagheads who intimidate you into giving them change.

This is the first place foreigners see when arriving by boat. Small wonder that nobody comes here on holiday.

BEN GROOM

31 OXFORD

Fortis est veritas (The truth is strong)

Population: **134 248**
Unemployment: **2.2%**
Violent crimes: **13.2 (per 1,000 per annum)**
% achieving 5 or more GCSE grades A-C: **98**
Famous resident: **Inspector Morse**

The beauty, prosperity and inspirational intellectual atmosphere of Oxford make it the most appealing of all English cities. Unfortunately, they come at the expense of dumping most of the poorer sections of the community in large, desperate estates.

At first glance Oxford appears to be the ideal English city. It's the beautiful home to one of the world's most distinguished universities, with a thriving centre and lush green spaces draped over a winding river.

Travel further afield though and you realise that this harmony is achieved thanks to the ghettoisation of large sections of the community, as the working classes are forced to live miles from the town in some of Europe's largest – and most notorious – housing estates. Like Blackbird Leys.

Blackbird Leys was where I grew up, and my childhood years revolved around the notion, dispensed from my Nan, that by living there we were suffering purgatory early, and would head straight for the highest reaches of heaven in our afterlife. Well, you had to believe something.

It wasn't just the row upon row of tiny matchbox houses, the serf's square of garden, the dogshit smeared along the dreary pot-holed roads. It wasn't even the fact that Blackbird Leys had been built on top of Oxford's sewers and that the air was constantly permeated with a heady mixture of decomposing waste.

It wasn't the melancholy; the look on people's faces as they formed an untidy

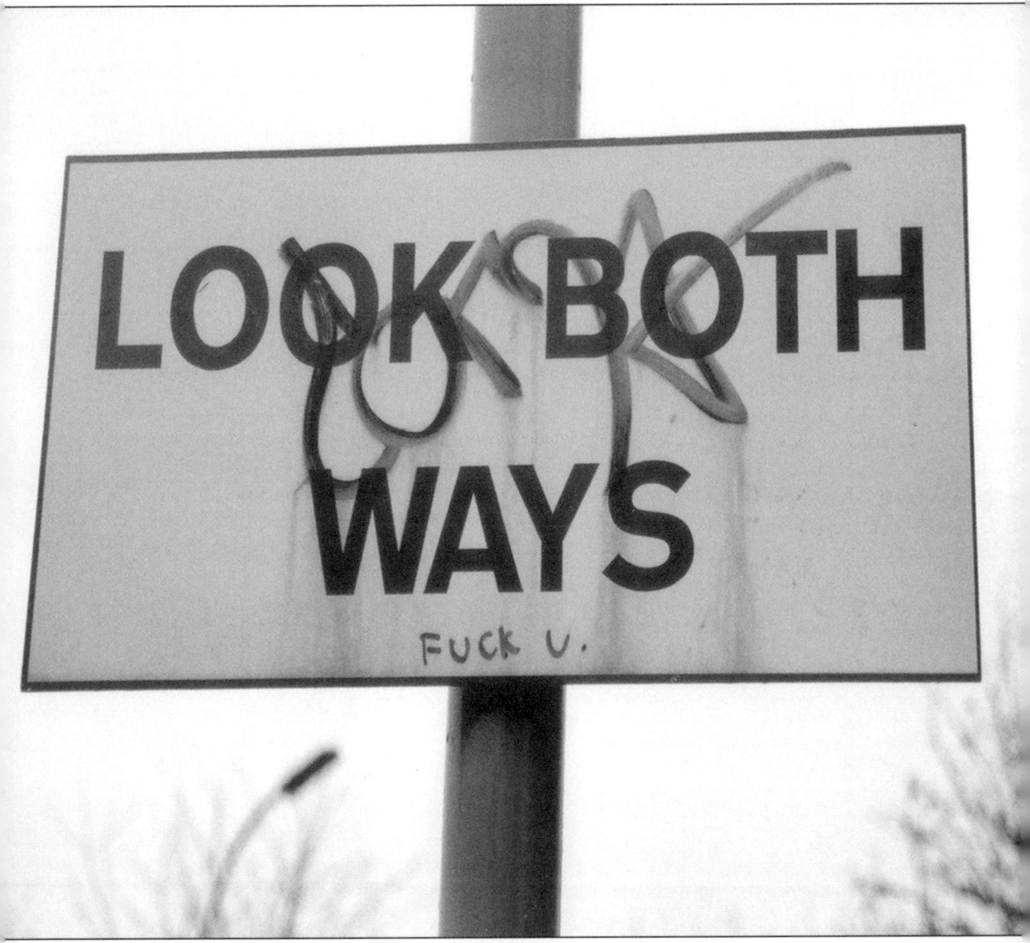
LOOK BOTH
WAYS
FUCK U.

'RAPE ALLEY',
BLACKBIRD LEYS

queue outside the post office, waiting for a giro that wouldn't quite buy enough food. Not the snot-face kiddies screaming hungrily in their buggies, or the sullen mothers hastily pulling a ragged piece of tissue from their pockets to wipe the little shithead's nose. The black-eyes worn like make-up, the low-level apathy seeping into everyone's bones.

It wasn't any of that. It was us, the kids: we were the worst thing. We happily committed unspeakable atrocities. Whether it was terrorising the local loonies – Mental Martha, Electric Mary, Demented Fred – setting fire to bins or spray-painting obscenities on to doors, whatever it was, we excelled at it, turning the sunset into curfew time for most.

Other kids I knew stole our neighbours' cars and raced them around the dingy estate roads. They badmouthed defenceless pensioners and pickpocketed people so poor the loss of money meant hunger for a week. They were young, unaccountable and blithely transformed the melancholy of the adults into palpable, stinging pain, as they dully watched them traverse the same old road, to the same old destiny.

That destiny sentenced most to curtailed school careers, teenage pregnancies, a lifetime of menial work and to purgatory in that shithole, Blackbird Leys.

No dreaming spires here. Tourists, enter at your peril.

ELOISE MILLAR

30 PETERHEAD
Veritas vincit (Truth conquers)

Population: **17,500**
Famous residents:
In the 1970s model Twiggy went to Peterhead to make a documentary about oil. Prince Charles once visited. That's about it

Lurking 35 miles north of Aberdeen, Peterhead has the dubious honour of having more churches per head of population than anywhere else in the UK. It has, in fact, more churches than hotels and pubs combined.
Instead of drink and drugs, the way to rebel against your parents is to take up Satanism. The News of the World dubbed the place the Satanism capital of Scotland. Peterhead is home to one of the most notorious high security prisons in Britain.

BRUCE MURRAY

29 TINTERN

**Population:
30,000**
**Famous residents:
Wordsworth (fleetingly)**

Tintern Abbey. It must be said that Wordsworth's famous "Lines" were composed "A Few Miles Above" it. He couldn't stand the godforsaken town either.
GRACE KLINE

28 MIRFIELD

Fruges Ecce Paludis
(Behold The Fruits Of The Swamp)

Population: **15,000**
Famous residents: **Patrick Stewart**

Situated at the shoddy end of West Yorkshire's textile belt, Mirfield has but two claims to fame:
1) The River Calder, which cuts through the town like a jet of piss through a festering turd, was once the most polluted in the country.
2) Patrick Stewart (Captain Picard in Star Trek) attended the main secondary school. He returns every few years to a rapturous reception from the kids who have just spent their break beating up the geeky trekkie kid.

There is also the canal which flows adjacent to the river, and the insalubrious wasteland therein. Abandoned cotton mills and the sewage works, which burned for five months a few years ago while the council tried to work out how to release the growing methane pressure, add to the general doom and gloom of the area.

I could go on, but the dog's just come back from a walk by the canal and we have to de-louse him.
JOSHUA

PHOTO: KEVIN PARR

"MY KIND OF TOWN.."
(SIGH) 'TWAS EVER THUS!
HOW THE FUCK COULD IT HAVE BEEN? THE BLACK DEATH'S ONE THING; POST INDUSTRIAL SOUL DEATH IS ANOTHER.
GWYN

27 HORSHAM
Proudly we serve

....

Population: **120,000**
Famous residents: **Serial killer Fred West, Jimmy Hill, Shelley**

....

Horsham is a No Fun Zone run by old conservatives for old conservatives. The fact that it was the second largest Conservative majority in the last General Election is entirely incidental, if somewhat damning in itself.

When the town elders were faced with applications for planning permission for a nightclub they responded with the priceless statement, 'The dance floor in the community centre in Roffey is entirely sufficient for our needs.'

Horsham appears to be the perennial winner of Southeast in Bloom, a fair indication of where the council's priorities for the town lie. Shall we spend money on decent sporting or leisure facilities? No, let's make the town look like the fallout from Ground Force ... minus the ever-tempting Charlie Dimmock.

Horsham is the head office for Royal & Sun Alliance, one of the UK's biggest insurers. Says it all really.

ANDY PALMER

26 HAYLING ISLAND

Population: 16,000
Famous residents: Two members of 70s prog rock group Gentle Giant, some guy who once appeared in a Kentucky Fried Chicken advert

Mostly populated by the over seventies, Hayling is the final destination of choice for wealthy people waiting to die.

In the 1980s, the local council decided the beaches were far too attractive so shipped in tons of stones to scatter over the once golden sand, rendering any hope of beach-based amusement impossible.

There is a funfair, consisting mostly of attractions bought from around the country when they were due to be condemned. Until recently the fair was banned from playing any form of music by the local residents, lest it drown out the sound of terrified screams of doomed children as their death-trap roller-coaster cars come rattling off the rails at the peak of the ride and send them hurtling into the English Channel ...

Hayling Island, the favoured holiday resort of people from Reading.

ANON

57

25 IPSWICH
Opus Nostrum Dirige
(Direct our work)

Population: 117,000
Unemployment: 3%
Violent crimes: 15.8
(per 1,000 per
annum)
% achieving 5 or
more GCSE grades A-C: 56.5

Hideous concrete monoliths overshadow the potentially attractive centre of this once thriving market town. The spiritual home for low slung Vauxhall Novas equipped with alloy wheels, Ipswich has a uniquely unbalancing effect on its more sensitive inhabitants. Like fellow Crap Towns, Leiston and Aldeburgh, it lies far too close for comfort to the Sizewell nuclear reactors.

When I was young I lived in Martlesham Heath and Ipswich was where you went if you wanted to go out. The last bus back from Ipswich left at ten p.m. I would go into town in the evening and watch my friends arrive. As I got into the town centre, me heart would always sink. It felt like the entire town was having an Everything Must Go sale. It felt like you could constantly hear country and western music, even when all you could really hear were people revving cars at traffic lights. I got that sinking feeling you get from seeing a single, discarded shoe in a gutter and you wonder how it got there (did he hop home?).

Sometimes my mum would drive out and pick me up on a Friday night, but I'd still ask her to come at ten. I never wanted to stay out any later. It's not like I would have been missing anything. At all. I would wait for her in front of a kebab shop (I've forgotten its name), opposite the Odeon (decaying), near the pub that served the over-twelves. There was a concrete slope there that led to a kind of pillar, about eight feet tall. I would climb up to the top and sit down. It was like a big high horse. That was the part of the evening I always enjoyed most.
ANDREW POET

TALK OF THE TOWN
I've lived on the outskirts for 15 years. Whenever I venture in, it's a totally depressing experience. Recently I walked into a wine bar at

ALL IPSWICH PHOTOS: SAM JORDISON

TUNNEL OF
LOVE, IPSWICH

7.30 pm to be told 'we've run out of wine'. Worth a trip if you want your life to bottom out.

All the guys in Ipswich wear black leather jackets and have short, cropped hair. The town centre looks like it's about to fall down in the next storm. All the pubs play exactly the same music day in day out – that half-assed clubbing thud thud crap that no one can talk over. Which is just as well, in a place where "coo" and "ugh" make up 90% of the vocabulary.

What's most depressing is that no one moves away – 'I's not goin' nowhere's else – they's all weird.'

MIKE

24 LEISTON

Population: 5,500
Unemployment: 3.4%
Violent crimes: 5.5
(per 1,000 per annum)
% achieving 5 or more GCSE grades A-C: 53
Famous residents: Will Self (briefly)

Leiston (aka Leiston-cum-Sizewell) is a manufacturing town where little is nowadays manufactured. A blot on the beautiful Suffolk countryside, it lies in the fallout zone of two nuclear power stations.

What distinguishes Leiston is its proximity to the two Sizewell reactors. I would swim in the waters around the station, warmed to a tepid tropical temperature by the heat of the core. My housemate swore by their restorative powers, as if it were an industrial Lourdes.
Although this wing of

ALL LEISTON PHOTOS: SAM JORDISON

Suffolk is patronised by the great media clans (both the Freuds and the Waughs maintain compounds further up the coast, the fruit of generations of nepotism), Leiston is quite beneath the moneyed crowd. There are no crappy shops selling 'crafts' knocked out by skittish Sloanes still recovering from their nervous breakdown.

No doubt the constant presence of Sizewell's tessellated white dome, looming on the horizon like a compound eye, prevented gentrification. There is a palpable atmosphere of conspiracy and evil, recalling Nigel Kneale's Quatermass serials of the Fifties. When a friend came to visit, I convinced him that the Butcher's Arms in Knodishall was merely a front for an opium-processing operation. Opium poppies grow wild in the area, and the prefabricated feel of the bar leant my outrageous lie plausibility. He still cites his visit to Leiston as the main cause of his subsequent psychological difficulties.

MATTHEW DE ABAITUA

IDLER ROVING REPORTER'S VERDICT

I went to Leiston on a freezing January day and cycled out to the eerie beach by Sizewell. I put my hand in the sea. It was disconcertingly warm. A man from Greenpeace later told me that this was 'a very brave' thing to do.

I now know that I can blame Leiston if I die of hand cancer.

When I got back to the town, a police helicopter was practising manoeuvres on the scruffy playing fields. Everyone in the town was standing around staring. They were acting like this was the

SIZEWELL BEACH. THE WATER IS WARM. THE FISH KEEP CHANGING SEX. IT'S WEIRD.

most interesting thing that had happened there for years.

It probably was.

Two men hurried past me. I heard one asking 'Do you reckon we can nick it?'

All the while the insistent wind howled in from Siberia. And there was the steady whine of Sizewell. I soon filtered out the sound, but the humming still permeated my subconscious, just as the radiation was seeping into my bones.

I don't want to go to Leiston again.

SAM JORDISON

ACCIDENT WAITING TO HAPPEN

The old square hulk of Sizewell A and the £2.46 billion dome of Sizewell B dominate the skyline in Leiston. Since its opening in 1995 Sizewell B alone has produced more than 210 tonnes of highly radioactive waste and about 10 per cent of the potential capability of wind farms off the coast of nearby East Anglia.

According to Greenpeace activist Rob Gueterbock, Sizewell B 'is easier to get into than a Norwich nightclub'. And he should know because he and 19 others broke into the nuclear site using 'a pair of wire cutters'. They occupied the control rooms and climbed onto the roof, waiting for 25 minutes before security even got close to them.

Should anyone decide to take advantage of this lax security for evil ends, Leiston, Aldeburgh and Ipswich will all be within the 35-mile fallout zone and London is just downwind.

At least residents of Leiston can take some comfort from the fact that their local police station holds a large supply of potassium iodide tablets. Not too much comfort though, because, as Armageddon expert Chas Newkey-Burden (the author of Nuclear Paranoia) explains, although the pills stop the thyroid taking in too much radiation, 'they're fuck all use for everything else. Taking potassium iodide when your village has turned into a radioactive mosh-pit is a bit like taking an aspirin when your head's on fire.'

SIZEWELL B AND SIZEWELL A

Nobody, but nobody has ever had good sex in Aldeburgh. You can tell just by walking around this flinty town.

Most people here are visiting older relatives, and we know what a suppres-

23 ALDEBURGH

Population: 1,000
Unemployment: 1.4%
Violent crime: 5.5
(per 1,000 per annum)
Famous residents:
Benjamin Britten

A beautiful town by a poetically bleak shingle beach on the Suffolk coast. A good setting for the M.R. James ghost story, 'A Warning to the Curious'. Blighted with more officious signs and odious conservatives per square inch than anywhere in the country.

sant effect that has on even the healthiest drives. The old people themselves, they've come to Aldeburgh because their sex life is over, and the young people who live here have to go outside the town boundary to begin to feel horny.

Sexual courage fails you in this terrible place. You could try doing it in the sea, but it's always cold – go further up the beach to Leiston/Sizewell to swim in the warm outflow. Even if you could stay in a hotel here, rather than with your Gran, there would be nothing here, nothing to stimulate the sexual appetite.

Eat sprats yes, go to a windswept boot sale on the side of the marshes, despair at the tangible class-divide, park your car wonkily sideways on the main street, get dragged off to church, or buy a white cardie from the charity shop, but forget getting laid. It just ain't gonna happen.

DAISY EVANS

IDLER ROVING REPORTER'S VERDICT

After visiting Leiston I cycled on through lovely countryside to Aldeburgh. It was beautiful, but cold. All the shops faced away from the sea. Everything was shut. Everywhere I looked, there was a strict instruction. 'Do not paddle here.' 'Do NOT let your dog walk here.' 'This is private property, strictly no admittance.' 'Do not put nappies into this bin.' 'Under NO circumstances may you take the brown chairs out of the restaurant and into the street.'

SAM JORDISON

22 BRIGHTON

Population: 247,817
Unemployment:
3.7%
Violent crimes: 16.8
(per 1,000 per
annum)
% achieving 5 or more
GCSE grades A-C: 45.6
Famous residents: Chris
Eubank, Julie Burchill,
Fatboy Slim, Zoë Ball

The home of the nearest beach to London, Tory conferences and endless media types, Brighton trades on a reputation for cool based on out-of-date trip-hop, big trainers and bad facial hair. The town's most beautiful landmark has been allowed to disappear into the sea and it's as seedy today as it was when Graham Greene made it the home of the ultra-violent Pinky in Brighton Rock.

I lived in Brighton for ten years. On the first evening of my residence there I took a stroll along the seafront at around 7 pm with my wife and our then one-year-old child. We admired the extravagance of the architecture and the beauty of the sunlight striking the rooftops (a peculiar quality of light I have only seen in Brighton) and congratulated ourselves on having chosen such an uplifting place in which to bring up our family.

Then a huge, ragged and wild-eyed man rushed up to us, waved a long and ugly-looking knife and demanded my wallet, before collapsing to the ground and passing out in a pool of his own vomit. That evening turned out to be an uncanny trailer for our next ten years in the town, which continued to delight, frighten, exhilarate and revolt us by turns.

I wouldn't live there again.

PAUL RICHARDSON

A TALE OF TWO CITIES

Brighton seems to labour under the misapprehension that it is Barcelona, a collective illusion reinforced by the constant crowing from the

CRAP TOWN TRIVIA *Dr Johnson, renowned for his love of England's capital, said that Brighton, now known as London-by-sea, 'is dull'. He called the town 'The World's End'.*

council about being a 'beautiful city by the sea'.

Half of it is dirty, noisy and packed to the gunnels with self-important superficial nasty young fashion victims with walkie-talkies with 'ironic' ringtones. These are the students, 'new media' and itinerant soi-disant shitneck pseudo-intellectuals.

The rest is an ordinary grimy Southeast town with council estates and young mums with lovebites and screaming kids and cod-eyed young men drenched in aftershave and cheap gold. They roam up and down the seafront on a Friday night, looking for someone from the other half to smack in the mouth.

JAMES

ALL BRIGHTON PHOTOS: RACHEL POULTON

CRAP TOWN TRIVIA A local support group has been trying to restore Brighton's lovely West Pier for more than two decades. Surprisingly, they have met with considerable local opposition, not least from the company that owns the town's other pier. A legal challenge was launched against the restoration project after it received £1.7million from the National Lottery in 1998. In February 2003, planning permission was finally given to go ahead with repairs. Within a month, a fire broke out, causing irreparable damage.

THE WEST PIER
BEFORE THE FIRE

IN DEFENCE OF BRIGHTON

Brighton and Hove is a City of a quarter of million people. Historically it is the premier seaside resort in England but the two boroughs which now make up the city of Brighton and Hove recognised during the 1960s that relying as a main part of the local economy on the traditional two week holiday trade was an insecure way of planning for the future. While tourism remains an important part of the local economy over the last thirty years our role as an International Conference Centre, the home to two popular Universities and the centre of a regional High Tech and Multi Media industry has helped to ensure a greater and more varied basis for economic buoyancy than has been experienced by some other traditional seaside towns.

The NHS and American Express have become other major employers across the city although, as happened in many other parts of the UK, because of policies pursued by the government in the 80s and early 90s a once thriving engineering sector has declined.

For many visitors to the city and local residents the Palace Pier remains a major attraction visited by some four million people a year. The Royal Pavillion, a unique oriental palace built in the 1820s as a summer home for the then Prince Regent, is another major attraction.

Brighton can also claim to have the widest variety of cafés, restaurants and bars outside London...

Like any vibrant and vital urban area with a diverse economy Brighton and Hove has its problems many of them problems shared with other parts of the South East - these include high house prices...

I am sorry that your correspondents don't like Brighton and Hove, I suspect that they would find the sorts of things that they object to anywhere they chose to live or visit.

DAVID LEPPER, LABOUR AND CO-OPERATIVE MEMBER OF PARLIAMENT

WELCOME TO HELL.
YEAH, YEAH... EVERYONE GOES ON ABOUT THE BOILING SHIT PITS, ..AND THE NEVERENDING VERY SEVERE PAIN... BUT NO ONE GOES ON TO MENTION OUR NEWLY RESTORED WEST PIER, OR THE MONO-RAIL...
GWYN

PHOTO: JULIA HEMBER

has been demolished to make way for five identical boxes; the large house opposite the marsh land – a veritable House of Usher – has given way to eight ugly, red brick, £750,000 monstrosities of blandness.

I went back recently. The place still had the insufferable smugness and bigotry one associates with the Range-Rover-driving classes. There were still no shops worth visiting, but now there was no green to speak of either. Housing estates proliferate around the race track like frogs around a pond. There is a three-week waiting list to get in one of the local pubs for Sunday lunch, and the bill will probably require you to remortgage your house.

Painful as it is, I have been forced to admit that the place where I was born and grew up is crap.

JAMIE BELL

20 DIDCOT

Population: **25,000**
Unemoployment: **1.7%**
Violent crimes: **4.1 (per 1,000 per annum)**
% achieving 5 or more GCSE grades A-C: **56**
Famous residents: **None**

The town exists because of a split, a void: the railway junction between the London–West coast and Oxford lines. This void infiltrates all aspects of the town. Resolutely ugly in spite of the beautiful countryside that it lies in, Didcot is growing out of control. Its grey mass spreads out rapidly, showing as much respect to the surrounding greenery as a malignant tumour does for a pair of lungs.

Didcot was created in the 1950s with the then (and still) novel town-planning concept of a one-sided high street. Empty shops on one side face houses on the other, which ensures no atmosphere on the high street and no privacy for the residents.

Didcot has in recent years been the subject of large-scale, completely unplanned expansion: a developer sprawl of orange brickwork and fake Victoriana (which, having been created in the twentieth century, Didcot otherwise completely lacks), with no connection to the dead high street but easy access to the out-of-town superstore.

There are no cultural facilities.

Didcot's saving grace (and she is graceful) is the power station, a cathedral scale beacon in the old flood plains of the Thames, with elegant and beautifully laid out cooling towers. Fortunately this can be appreciated for miles around and there should be no reason to visit the town itself.

WILLIAM SMALLEY

CORRECTION

Didcot was not created in the 1950s – it dates back as a hamlet to medieval times, although its expansion came about when the people of the town of Abingdon (then county town of Berkshire) refused to allow the Great Western Railway to go through their own town. Brunel built a station in the then-village of Didcot.

Didcot expanded during the 1930s with a

whole estate of tiny houses with huge gardens being built at the south side of the town for the Welsh navvies then working on the railway. Then in the 1950s the awful town centre (well, the Broadway) was built, as well as a couple more large estates to the west side of the town. Since the 1980s more and more has been added.

A large proportion of the people who live in Didcot are not here during office hours, as they only moved here because house prices in London (or Reading) are so high. This has in turn pushed the price of property in Didcot to be ridiculously high for a town where you wouldn't live if you had any choice in the matter.
SCOTT EARLE

....

IN DEFENCE OF DIDCOT

This is an unwarranted and unfair attack on Didcot. But at least it gives me the chance to stand up for the town. I know from talking to people who have lived here for many years

ALL DIDCOT PHOTOS: SAM JORDISON

that the town has a very strong community and people enjoy living here.

In fact Didcot is a growing town, which shows it must be doing something right. More than 5000 people have come to live here in the last few years. And in which other British town will you find a Nuclear Scientist, a Space Programme Researcher, a Formula 1 Car Designer, a Train Driver, a Shepherd, a Stockbroker and a Pig Breeder? When the long-awaited town centre development takes place, Didcot will be an even better place to live.

Didcot has an enviable quality of life. On almost every quality of life indicator, such as levels of crime and employment, Didcot outperforms the rest of the country. Didcot Girls' School was the best performing school this year in Oxfordshire, in terms of its improvement.

Didcot is centrally located and people can commute to Oxford in just 15 minutes, and get to London in just 45. But it is also in the heart of the countryside,

JUVENILE ON MAIN STREET, DIDCOT

with the Ridgeway nearby, lovely villages on its outskirts, the White Horse at Uffington, Lambourn, Henley, the Chilterns. For the literary minded the final resting places of famous names are nearby. Agatha Christie in Cholsey, George Orwell in Sutton Courtney and Jerome K. Jerome in Ewelme.

Didcot has the world-famous Didcot Railway Centre Museum, home of the Great Western Society and its unique collection of Great Western Railway steam engines, coaches, wagons, buildings and small relics. The Didcot power station is both loved and hated – but there is no doubt that for the last thirty years it has provided a striking landmark for the town, as well as supplying a large part of the electricity for the Southeast of England. And of course we are home to The Gunners – the nickname for Didcot Town Football Club after the Woolwich Arsenal moved here in the First World War.

EDWARD VAIZEY, PROSPECTIVE CONSERVATIVE CANDIDATE FOR WANTAGE

19 WOLVERHAMPTON
Out of darkness cometh light

Population: **242,000**
Unemployment: **5%**
Violent crimes: **25.2 (per 1,000 per annum)**
% achieving 5 or more GCSE grades A-C: **42.4**
Famous residents: **Slade bass guitarist Jimmy Lea, Eric Idle, Lenny Henry**

Wolverhampton finally managed to prove that it was more than just a suburb of Birmingham by becoming Britain's newest city in 2001. That doesn't mean that this former industrial powerhouse hasn't seen far better days.

CRAP TOWN TRIVIA In the 18th century Wolverhampton was a world centre for the production of jewellery made out of steel. It didn't last. Before the industry collapsed, however, local man John Worralow was appointed steel jeweller to King George III. King George III was as mad as a bag of snakes.

Wolverhampton was made a city in 2001. As the nation shrugged, TV pictures were beamed into every home, showing Wolverhampton's town crier (who reasoned that a testimony to Sixties concrete renewal required a town crier?) announcing this momentous event to at least six interested residents gathered on Dudley Street in the pissing rain.

The most attractive thing about Wolverhampton was the multi-storey carpark on School Street, the roof level of which used to offer rural vistas of Staffordshire, Shropshire and the Wrekin. However, the council knocked it down in the Nineties.

Unemployment in Wolverhampton is staggeringly high and the city is so divided along class and racial lines that it is hardly a city at all but a collection of tribal groupings.

In the evenings, the smell of hops from Banks' Brewery permeates the town like the stench of a trapped animal slowly decaying in a drain pipe.

MICHAEL THOMPSON

18 PETERBOROUGH
Upon this rock

Population: 156,000
Unemployment: 3%
**Violent crimes: 14.9 (per
1,000 per annum)**
**% achieving 5 or more
GCSE grades A–C: 42.9**
Famous residents: **Johnny Vaughn,
Jimmy Saville, Geoff Capes, Maxim
from The Prodigy**

Peterborough was a small town expanded by the New Town initiative of the 1960s. Whatever charm this modest fenland community once had was soon buried under fifty million tons of concrete. Which is not to say that the new Peterborough lacks character – just that its character is that of a colourless middle-manager.

Take a wander through these uninspiring streets, perhaps pausing to browse the chain-stores and discount warehouses. As night falls, choose between a brandname pub or a generic nightclub – although you'll be lucky to get in wearing those shoes. And who better to rally civic pride than a team of perennial underachievers like Peterborough United? At least there is a big Cathedral, where lost souls can pray to be delivered from this hellhole.

Every time that Peterborough gets attacked in print (which is often), the council's rapid response unit mobilises and turns its fire on the critics. They declare with Stalinist zeal that Peterborough has the highest quality of life anywhere in the Western world. Well, it's what they're paid for, but they might like to reflect why they've had so much practice over the years.

JAMES OLIVER

17 LONDON

Population: **7million**
Unemployment: **7%**
Violent crimes:
90.2 (per 1,000 per annum)
Famous residents:
Mike Reid, Chas 'n' Dave

Since the Romans named it Londinium in AD 43 our capital has been burned by Boudicca, stormed by the Vikings, infested by the Black Death, licked almost to extinction by fire, and bombed to smithereens. In modern times the biggest threat to its existence is its affluence. The lifeblood of the city – teachers, nurses, ambulance drivers, firemen and bin men – are moving out in droves because of insane property prices and ludicrous rents. Still, before they all leave, London does have a lot to offer: great pubs, clubs, restaurants, cinemas, theatres, parks, museums … It's all there, providing you can afford to get in.

It's over-rated. It's over-priced. It does not swing. It does, moreover, have lots of rain. It has a preponderance of unpleasant locals in every walk of life. And worst of all, one's friends go there in search of fame and fortune, only to vanish completely, trapped in a terrible vortex of debt and job insecurity, and one never sees them again.

IAIN SCOTT

BRIDGE & PRIMROSE HILL PHOTOS: DAN KIERAN

CHAS 'N DAVE

TIRED OF LONDON

First off only 40 per cent of Londoners are born there so the idea of a 'preponderance of locals' is preposterous. It's the mad influx that keeps the place full up and expensive but there's always a price for success. It is the same influx that keeps the place alive. Where else would you get primary schools with pupils from 78 countries?

London is one of the most cosmopolitan cities in the world and most areas have a large mix of race and class. There are very few ghettoes in London and cultural entertainment is global in origin. As for 'swinging', you're better off going to Basildon for that sort of party ...

JOHN HASLER

ARCHWAY,
'SUICIDE' BRIDGE

Like Dr Johnson said 'He who tires of London tires of life itself.' Yes, it is expensive but that's 'cos it's absolutely brilliant and well worth it. Yes, housing is overpriced but it is just obeying basic economics – people are willing to pay to live in London because it's so great.

NICK J

TIRED OF JOHNSON

That Johnson quote was written when Southwark was still a village in Surrey.

Far better is: 'that great foul city of London there ... rattling, growling, smoking, stinking ... a ghastly heap of fermenting brickwork, pouring out poison at every pore' (John Ruskin).

JIM

PRIMROSE HILL

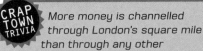

CRAP TOWN TRIVIA More money is channelled through London's square mile than through any other European city. A recent report by the Department of the Environment, Transport and Regions found that London contains 60 per cent of England's most deprived housing estates. Another report, commissioned by London Mayor Ken Livingstone, found that 53 per cent of London's children are being brought up below the government's official poverty line.

He who tires of London tires of going to a bar in Clapham that only serves bottled beers at £5, and which looks like someone's front room.

SIMON SHARP

DR JOHNSON WRITES

London is a collection of small, soulless towns, some of which are linked by an unreliable tube. The result is a combination of the small-minded attitudes of a provincial town and the urban alienation of a big city.

This Dr Johnson still loves life but is tired of London.

DR (DAVID) JOHNSON

A GENTLEMAN WRITES

I remember Ken Livingstone's mayoral campaign and him triumphantly declaring that London was the most beautiful city in the world. I wonder when he last walked up Blackstock Road.

**JEREMY DYSON
(THE LEAGUE OF GENTLEMEN)**

16 ISLINGTON LONDON
Deus Per Omnia (God in everything)

Population: **176,000**
Unemployment: **6%**
Violent Crimes: **30.9**
% achieving 5 or more
GCSE grades A–C: **32.9**
Famous residents: **Tony Blair**

Islington is most notable for a high street with bars populated by men with facial hair and women with wrinkled faces. Everyone smells of beans and marijuana. Nowhere else in the world can you come across so many people in their thirties dressed as teenagers.

Endless streets of identical Victorian terraces, lived in by Jacks and Chloës who go to Arsenal, eat pie 'n' chips and speak in half-words. But this is merely a stepping stone to the next staging post in the middle-class diaspora (Hampstead) where they return to their natural foods, accents and dress-codes. Bastards.

ANDREW BAILLIE

15 CROYDON LONDON

Ad summa nitamur (Let's try our best)

Population: **330,688**
Unemployment: **3.7%**
Violent Crimes: **18.7 (per 1,000 per annum)**
% achieving 5 or more GCSE grades A-C: **44.9**
Famous residents: **Derek Bentley - one of the last men to be hanged in Britain**

West Croydon bus station serves as a kind of halfway house for the mental health ward at Mayday Hospital. The floor is littered with KFC chicken bones, like some ancient caveman dwelling, and the air stinks of piss and Vaseline. From here, if you avoid being chopped into bite-size chunks and stuffed into a secondhand suitcase, you can

make your way up to the high street. Be careful not to look anyone in the eye or smile; this is often misconstrued and could lead to verbal and even physical abuse. 'Whatchoo lookin' at you fuckin' cunt?' will be the last thing you hear before you're poked in the eye with a halfsnouted cigarette.

SARAH JANES

CRAP TOWN TRIVIA

Croydon has gifted two phrases to the slang lexicon:

Croydon-facelift *n.*
Hair that is scraped back so tight into a pony tail that it pulls back the wearer's cheek bones.

Pram-face *n.*
Young celebrity who looks like she ought to be pushing a pram around Croydon. e.g. Baby Spice.

PHOTO: DAVID JANES

14 ST JOHN'S WOOD LONDON

Famous residents: Liam Gallagher, Patsy Kensit, Jerry Springer, Lady Bienvenida Buck (scandal-causing wife of a Tory MP, now reduced to making appearances on Kilroy), Paul McCartney, Mel Smith

I was walking down St John's Wood High Street on a cold, bright January Sunday. It's a beautiful part of London. Everything seems unusually low down which makes for a nice change. So the six policemen, who were pounding up and down the road in a severe state of agitation, looked somewhat out of place. I overheard one say 'fucking arrogant bastards' to his colleague.

There isn't much space for cars on St John's Wood High Street. There are just two narrow lanes with parking meters dotted all the way along either side of the road. The traffic problem is exacerbated by herds of oversized Land Rovers.

The owners of these beasts double park wherever they like. When I was there, they were just sticking their flashing lights on and walking off, leaving anyone behind completely stuck because someone else had done exactly the same thing on the other side. And it wasn't the odd one or two, this was happening all the way up and down the road. The policemen were deeply exasperated. Every time someone stopped, put their hazard lights on and began climbing out of their car, one of the red-faced boys in blue would rush towards the offender and shout; 'Get back in there now! Don't stop here! Move it now!'

I saw one woman receiving this entirely justified outburst after double parking outside a Gap kids shop. She raised her eyebrows and pulled her head back a few inches in surprise.

She calmly closed the car door behind her and smiled at the policeman. As she walked towards the curb she said over her shoulder – in a tone which she genuinely seemed to mean to be helpful: 'Fine me if you like. I can afford it.'

DAN KIERAN

PHOTO: DAN KIERAN

CAR PARK, ST JOHN'S WOOD

13 CROUCH END

LONDON

**Famous residents:
Dave Stewart,
Fran Healy from
Travis, Damian
from The Damned**

The rent; the roll-ups; the obsession with property; the tiny boutiques and their tiny girl staff; the kite shops; the actors; the authors; the docusoap film crews; the balding revolutionaries with their Amis-fixations; the charity muggers who want to be actors; the Upper Street overspill who think Wood Green's in Surrey; the tyranny of pesto; the minicab wars; the 4x4s; the red painted rooms with their twigs in jars; the hat-shops; the dogshit; its

vast self importance; the police chopper (why?); the village vibe (where?); the nu-metal pixies on the video shop counter; no decent pubs unless you're already drunk; the rootless residents who think they're locals; the resentful locals leaving for Enfield; the babies called Dylan in the juggernaut prams; that story about Dylan and the wrong Dave Stewart; the stumbling joggers; the inverted commas; the ley line myth; the smirking cynics having a go at the place; the beggars; the bus ticket machines; Nick Hornby; that Will Self short story; the clock tower that thinks it's Glastonbury Tor; the parking; the papers; the smell the hill the horror …

JON FORTGANG

THE DYLAN STORY FROM THE RIGHT DAVE STEWART

'When we were recording in London, Dylan arrived at my house, an hour late, all flustered. I asked what had happened and he said, well I rang the doorbell of number seven and this woman comes to the door, and I said, Is Dave here?, and she said, No, he's at work do you want to wait?

'So Dylan waits and thinks, that's strange, he told me to come round. And the woman's thinking, this is weird, he looks like Bob Dylan. So she rings up her husband and asks him, Did you invite Bob Dylan round to our house? The husband doesn't know what she's talking about and it turns out that Dylan has got the right number, but the wrong street.'

SOURCE: Q MAGAZINE

ALL CROUCH END PHOTOS: DAN KIERAN

12 STOCKPORT

Animo et fide (With courage and faith)

Population: **284,000**
Unemployment:
2.3%
Violent crimes: **11.9 (per 1,000 per annum)**
% achieving 5 or more GCSE grades A-C: **52.4**
Famous residents: **George Best ended his footballing career at Stockport County. Fred Perry, John Mahone**

Stockport is a typical Northwestern mill town made prosperous in the Industrial Revolution, but failing to maintain the same momentum since. It used to be a major millinery centre and a huge hat museum dominates its skyline.

Stockport is a town in South Manchester. Much of Engels' research for Marx's Communist Manifesto was based on the appalling working conditions in the town's hat mills. And to be honest it's gone downhill ever since.

The overriding 'look' for Stockport's locals is a shaven head with optional Fila cap/visor perched on top, a Reebok shellsuit, the legs of which are tucked into a pair of overpowering patterned socks and a pair of Rockport, Timberland or Kicker boots. Gold jewellery is popular, usually incorporating sovereigns and/or marijuana leaf motifs. The male uniform is fairly similar.

Anyone deviating from this universally accepted look faces daily verbal and physical abuse.

Entertainment includes avoiding being glassed in one of the town's many pubs, avoiding being stabbed on the infamous 192 bus and avoiding leaving your house as much as possible.

Merseyway precinct is the town's heart. If you do wish to buy anything from Woolworths, Argos or 'Everything For £1', avoid walking within a stone's throw of the second-floor balcony edge or you face a shower of gob, McDonald's fries and stones from the gangs of youths above.

Recent attempts to open an Amsterdam-style cannabis cafe were thwarted by local police.

CHARLIE HUNGERFORD AND SEAN ARNOLD

IN DEFENCE OF STOCKPORT

Last time we looked we were a Metropolitan borough of 127,000 homes occupied by 295,000 people, bordering Manchester, the Peak District National Park and the Cheshire Plain. We only just missed becoming a city in 2001, local education results are among the top nationally, and public satisfaction with Council services is above average. Some mills we do still have – but they're being turned into unusual attractions like the Hat Works, Britain's only museum of hats and hat wearing. And, from what we see, conditions in the many top companies in the borough, things have moved on quite a bit since Engels last visited!

With Merseyway Shopping Centre among the top retail centres in Greater Manchester, and boasting all the high street stores, there's not much call for the shellsuit look these days – though some of the Man United footballers

who've made Stockport their home might sport some kind of Kicker boots!

There are several local parks that have won awards and the Trans-Pennine Trail from Liverpool to Hull goes through Stockport. Good pubs and restaurants are dotted across the borough and we are on the doorstep of Manchester city centre.

We've nothing to be ashamed of!

STOCKPORT COUNCIL

CRAP TOWN TRIVIA *Stockport contains Europe's second largest brick-built structure, the Stockport Viaduct. This impressive artifice was featured in a TV campaign before the last general election to encourage people in the region to vote. Unfortunately the advert broadcast rather mixed messages and several hundred people turned up at the foot of the enormous structure thinking that that was where they should register.*

IT'S GRIM UP NORTH

11 PORTSMOUTH
Heaven's light our guide

Population: 186,700
Unemployment: 3%
Violent crime: 17.7
(per 1,000 per annum)
% achieving 5 or more GCSE grades A-C: 36.5
Famous residents: HG Wells, Freddie Mercury, Charles Dickens, Isambard Kingdom Brunel

'Pompey' is a good place to sail out of, a port used by no lesser men than Nelson, Captain Cook and Henry VIII. It's the second most densely populated area in Europe and apparently has one of the thickest populations.

Portsmouth may have one feature which could be considered redeeming: a beach. But then you realise that the beach is of course, being Portsmouthian, of the pebble variety, and therefore utterly useless. And the sea itself, being Portsmouthian, is of the brown variety. And not just in winter. It is brown, stinking and full of used condoms and needles all the year round. Holidaygoers to the seaside in Portsmouth rarely venture from their cars, and sit, glassy-eyed, flask of tea and soggy sandwich in hand, staring out at the grey horizon and wondering, presumably, how to end their lives.

On the architecture front, Portsmouth boasts many triumphs of the idiocy of the human spirit. The 'Tricorn', a shopping centre, is surely the ugliest concrete monstrosity on the face of the earth. The ABC cinema fell into disuse about two years ago, presumably because the punters became too depressed to leave their homes. Now a target for vandals, arsonists and drug addicts, looking at it pretty much sums up that gnawing, dripping feeling of dread, regret and panic that epitomises the town.
GARETH IRVINE

IN DEFENCE OF PORTSMOUTH
Many of the 5.5 million tourists who visit Portsmouth and pump around £230 million into the local economy every year agree on one thing – it's a vibrant city with a rich historical past and an exciting future.

PHOTO: RACHEL POULTON

The ultimate
shopping experience

Be inspired by a new

Some £50m of government SRB and private funding is being pumped into a city which has fast slipped from 44th to 119th in the national list of the country's most deprived places.

A city going nowhere with no cultural heritage – and a place which hasn't produced anyone worthy of note? We don't think so.

Charles Dickens, Isambard Kingdom Brunel (who both made the final list of ten in the BBC's search for the top Briton), Peter Sellers and ex-Prime Minister James Callaghan were all

CRAP TOWN TRIVIA Henry VIII watched from Portsmouth as the Mary Rose sank in 1545. The ill-fated Captain Bligh of the Bounty sailed from Pompey in 1787. Nelson left England from Portsmouth in 1805, on his way to Trafalgar and death.

CRAP TOWN TRIVIA *Portsmouth is currently the field for the sad yet ridiculous "kebab war". Several traders have been killed because of competition to land a prime spot on Portsmouth's meat street.*

Portsmouth-born. Sir Arthur Conan Doyle created Sherlock Holmes while he lived in the city. Rudyard Kipling also lived here. Olympic-medal winning athlete Roger Black, musician Joe Jackson and top BBC news presenter George Alagiyah are other ex-city lads who might argue that they've 'done good'.

The home of the Royal Navy boasts a maritime heritage centre which is the envy of the world, including HMS Victory, the new £14m Action Stations attraction, the Mary Rose and HMS Warrior 1860, Britain's first ironclad battleship.

Why not just walk along the four miles of seafront and watch superferries, hovercraft and catamarans jostle with modern warships and the colourful sails of windsurfers and yachts.

Who'd want to live here? Who wouldn't?

EXTRACT FROM A LONG LETTER FROM COUNCILLOR MIKE HANCOCK, EXECUTIVE MEMBER FOR ECONOMIC DEVELOPMENT AND TOURISM, PORTSMOUTH CITY COUNCIL

PHOTO: GARETH IRVINE

HACKNEY

Justitia turris nostra
(Justice is our tower or Our tower is righteous)

Population: **202,824**
Unemployment: **6.6%**
Violent crimes: **31.8 (per 1,000 per annum)**
% achieving 5 or more GCSE grades A-C: **31.3**
(4th from bottom in the country)
Famous residents: **Ray Winstone, Michael Caine, Harold Pinter, Throbbing Gristle (the band), Iain Sinclair, Jack The Ripper and Jarvis Cocker (until he left because he was fed up with being mugged)**

It's cheap, it's within easy commuting distance of central London, it has some of the best pubs and parks for miles around and it's the favoured hangout of some of the most important artists in Britain today. Hackney would be a great place to live – if only living there weren't so dangerous and dirty.

ALL HACKNEY PHOTOS: SAM JORDISON

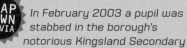

CRAP TOWN TRIVIA *In February 2003 a pupil was stabbed in the borough's notorious Kingsland Secondary School playground and rushed to hospital. The police searched the school and found three more weapons. When a concerned parent phoned the school to inform them he was withdrawing his son because they could not guarantee his safety, he was told: 'This is Hackney, sir. People do carry weapons.'*

Over the past few years the residents of the tragically deprived borough of Hackney have had to get used to wading through piles of litter. It has recently been revealed, to council tax payers' great surprise, that they are paying more for waste disposal services than everyone else in the country – even though their waste is so rarely disposed of. £19 million was paid to private contractors (in spite of the fact that an in-house council department bid £8.5 million for the same job).

Of course, the problems with litter are

CRAP TOWN TRIVIA

TOWER OF JUSTICE

Reported burglaries per 1,000 of population in Hackney are 14.8 – more than 11 times the national average. Reported thefts of vehicles stand at 13.8 per 1,000 of population – more than twice the national average. And most crimes in Hackney go unreported. Even so a week never goes by without at least one gruesome stabbing story in the Hackney Gazette. There have recently even been a couple of human skinnings.

UNDER SIEGE

In January 2003 Hackney ousted Hull from the dubious position of being the site of the longest siege in UK history with the 16 day stand-off between police and Eli Hall. Tragically Eli Hall died without smoking the weed his friend had hidden inside the skin of a KFC chicken and tried to smuggle past the police.

GUN HAPPY

A Hackney man died after a bullet came through a wall and hit him at a New Year's Eve party at the start of 2002. The bullet also killed a DJ, who it was originally fired at, travelling through his neck, and on into the next room. On the same night several people in Chimes nightclub received gun shot wounds when revellers began letting off rounds on the dance floor. A spokesman later attributed the shootings to 'high spirits'.

entirely unrelated to the corruption that has dogged Hackney in the past. Dodgy budgets and mysteriously disappearing money have been a part of life, from the 'cash for keys scandal' in the early Nineties, a key selling and housing benefit racket which cost millions of pounds, to the current investigations of Scotland Yard into a bogus grants payment scheme. Topping it all, the fraud department in the council itself has recently been under scrutiny for having its own fingers lodged in some very fishy pies.

Add to this a bunch of poll-rigging politicians (including two – Liberal and Tory – who were jailed for six months in 1998), Britain's worst school (Hackney Downs, now demolished after being declared 'beyond hope') and Accident and Emergency wards which one doctor pronounced as worse for gunshot wounds than Soweto. Lovely.

ELOISE MILLAR AND SAM JORDISON

CLARENCE ROAD, HOME TO RATS, CRACK DEALERS AND COMPILERS OF SHITTY URBAN BOOKS

9

BASINGSTOKE
Steadfast in service

ALL BASINGSTOKE PHOTOS: AARON EDWARDS

Population: **152,600**
Unemployment: **1.7%**
Violent crimes: **7.6 (per 1,000 per annum)**
% achieving 5 or more GCSE grades A-C: **53**
Famous residents: **Tanita Tikaram, Sarah Ferguson, Liz Hurley, Rick Parfitt from Status Quo**

Basingstoke was a small inoffensive market town until 1961 when it was chosen to receive London overspill. Now it's large and offensive.

The tallest building between London and New York is in Basingstoke: the Churchill Plaza. To my knowledge Basingstoke has absolutely no connection with Churchill whatsoever, but then I guess the Tanita Tikaram Plaza just sounds silly. It's an unnecessarily huge glass-fronted building which, along with a series of smaller but no less glazed buildings, earned Basingstoke the title of 'The Dallas of South England' in the Independent (alright, they were probably taking the piss).

Basingstoke's town centre at the time of writing resembles 'Ground Zero' on September 12th (they're in the middle of a multi-million pound refurbishment designed to draw shoppers away from Swindon). It was once dominated by the massive structure of Europe's ex-largest multi-storey carpark. This masterpiece of precast concrete sat imposingly over the main shopping area, lending the place an air of inner-city urban decay. In an attempt to improve the generally miserable image of the town, the council decided to cover the concrete with that white plastic stuff they use to make modern window frames. Well, they covered half of it anyway, randomly. They've now pulled the whole thing down, and I'll miss it. Maybe.

Basingstoke council have also invested several thousands of pounds on what it describes as 'modern' art. This includes a theatre/venue in the shape of an anvil (inspiringly named The Anvil), a six foot high ballerina, a pair of gates that don't actually lead anywhere, and two blokes holding large curved poles which if you squint resemble the arch that you always used to see Iraqi troops marching through on the news.

AARON EDWARDS

....

PUKE

A London overspill town. Everything is mild. It is not a place of dark despair or hardcore grimness like Hull or Slough. There are no vast, crime-ridden estates. Crime only extends as far as a few burnt-out cars dumped on the ring-road verges, and the terminally boring monochromatic graffiti that you can see during any train journey in England.

Arriving at the train station and

A DRIVE THROUGH BASINGSTOKE

M3, carpark, carpark, roundabout, carpark, roundabout, carpark, tart, roundabout M3.
Takes about three hours.
ANDY

CRAP TOWN TRIVIA

The arch of two enormous swords in Baghdad, built to celebrate victory in the Iran - Iraq war was actually cast in Basingstoke. The council, seeming to share the same taste in municipal architecture as Saddam Hussein, liked them so much they made one of their own.

WHICH IS WHICH?

The writer Jane Austen once became engaged to a Basingstoke resident. However, she thought better of it, and severed relationships with the hapless young man within 24 hours of getting attached.

walking out on to the front plaza is like getting out of a lift in the basement boiler room when you expected to get off in the plush ground-floor lobby. You face the end of the town's old shopping centre, which has just been extended via a totally inept merging with a brand new shopping centre that rivals Reading's and Portsmouth's emporia in its rich money-parting experience.

As with the majority of modern towns, there is the high street cluster of pubs all within

CRAP TOWN TRIVIA *The council attempted to make the grim shopping centre appear friendlier in the 1980s by adorning it with a huge legend 'Welcome To Basingstoke'. The letters were made out of lights. Occasionally some of the bulbs would explode and die, creating new messages such as 'We come to toke'. Now it just says 'Sainsburys'.*
PAUL HAMILTON

puking or bottle-throwing distance of each other. And the Basingstoke bouncers are uncommonly anal about footwear, but not about the quality of the actual people they are admitting.
M. BAILEY

DICKISH PUBLIC
ART, BASINGSTOKE

CRAP TOWN TRIVIA

One of Basingstoke's claims to fame is that the first train fatality occurred there. Some poor sod was decapitated. Considering how slowly steam engines moved, one wonders whether it was suicide.

PAUL HAMILTON

BASINGSTOKE HELPS OPEN DOORS

I've never been to Basingstoke, but I met a man who did. While staying at the Phillipe Starck-designed Paramount Hotel just off Times Square in New York, I felt sorry for the young guy whose job it was to open the door whenever anyone wanted to enter or leave. I stopped to chat, and offered my sympathy for having such a tedious job. He replied, 'I'm from Basingstoke – nothing's boring after that.'

PAUL RICHARDSON

HAN SOLO

Basingstoke sites the fact that the Churchill Plaza is the tallest building between London and New York as a claim to fame. Given that there is very little at all between London and New York, I think my claim that I once saw Harrison Ford on the tube is far more remarkable.

IAIN GOLDFINCH

HOUSE OF COMMONS
LONDON SW1A 0AA

25 February 2003

Dear Mr Kieran

Thank you for your fax of 18 February. I appreciated hearing from you and read your letter and the accompanying testimony with very great interest.

You tell me that you have been unable to find someone who is prepared to paint Basingstoke in a positive light. I do not believe that you have looked very far! An obvious starting point would have been the Borough Council and the elected Councillors who represent the various parts of the town.

Many jokes have been made about Basingstoke over the years and many people have tried to present the town in an unfavourable light. Neither the jokes nor the insults have much impact locally. Basingstoke is one of the most prosperous towns in the south of England and, by and large, Basingstoke residents count themselves fortunate.

Unlike so many other towns in the greater area, traffic flows relatively smoothly; not for us, for instance, the horrors of Winchester or Reading. Wider communication could hardly be better. The M3 is at our back door, the M4 within easy reach; so are Heathrow and Southampton airports. Over the years, Basingstoke has consistently enjoyed one of the highest levels of employment. The local economy is soundly-based and has also benefited enormously from inward investment.

The recently concluded redevelopment of Basingstoke's town centre was, at the time, the largest project of its kind in the United Kingdom. The new town centre at the very least matches anything of its kind to be found in the south of England. Leisure facilities in Basingstoke are excellent. The Haymarket Theatre thrives and the Anvil concert hall is a cultural centre of excellence. To crown it all, Basingstoke is within easy reach of idyllic Hampshire countryside. It is not surprising that the overwhelming majority of Basingstoke residents count their blessings.

Yours sincerely

Andrew Hunter

Andrew Hunter
Member of Parliament, Basingstoke

Member of Parliament, Basingstoke

AN OLD TOWN

BEXHILL-ON-SEA

8

Population: **42,000**
Unemployment: **2%**
Violent crimes: **13.4**
(per 1,000 per annum)
% achieving 5 or more GCSE grades A-C: **59.5**

The human equivalent of an elephant's graveyard, populated by people who have nothing left to do but die, Bexhill-On-Sea is a very English seaside town. And it smells of ammonia and cats.

PHOTO: SARAH JANES

118

CENTENARY
BEXHILL·ON·SEA
1902 ~ 2002

Referred to as God's Waiting Room affectionately by its inhabitants, who are mostly half way between the waiting room and the doctor's office, Bexhill-On-Sea is a place where you are forever being subjected to the velvety damp caresses of virtual cadavers, at bus stops, in cafes, on the street; the very essence of death permeates every molecule in the air. The whir of mobility carriages, the buzzing of hearing aids and the constant coughing and spluttering make your teeth grind. It has nothing; it is nothing, a shell of its former self perhaps. It is a town waiting to die, on a life-support machine, with no one prepared to do the decent thing and put a pillow over its head.

It drives you to drink port in the afternoon, which is actually rather nice, but nothing can be achieved whilst in its midst. You feel useless and hopeless and just when you feel it cannot get any lower, you drop another level and the port turns to Olde English and the afternoon turns to morning and you're forced to take a job in an old lady cafe to support your habit and then they make you take the deliveries to the old folk who can't get out and about like they used to. There is a constant smell of ammonia and cats and stewed tea in your nostrils and it seems as though their deathliness is in that smell and hence in you.

Everyone's heater's up full whack, everyone's TV likewise, sorrow and regret and lives lived out to the extremities. Lonely and miserable and longing to die. Doorbells go unanswered, chipped dinner plates turn cold on cold steps, curtains no longer opened. Time to move, time to move away, out of this world and into the next, out of the darkness and into the light ...
SARAH JANES

....

PERCHANCE TO DREAM

Growing up in Bexhill is like living life back to front. You're born into an environment where death is the next and only step, and you grow up in a world where old people are your bench-mark of normality.

I offer you two events from my boyhood in Bexhill. First, Bexhill was the only town in the UK where the cinema decided not to show E.T. when it first came out. They reasoned that everyone would have already seen it. Secondly, the local paper once announced that a dinosaur footprint had been found in the clay rocks off Galley Hill. That Sunday we went to stand and stare, like many others. A week later it emerged

PHOTO: GAVIN PRETOR-PINNEY

that, actually, that footprint was already known about. It appeared every ten years or so, depending on the tides.

Both those stories might not say anything directly, but they sum up exactly the way life manages both to pass Bexhill by and stand still at the same time – a warping of relativity that would have Einstein spinning in his grave. Or at least going for a gentle stroll along the seafront.

I'm in a deckchair at the De La Warr Pavilion. The band may start playing again, later, I think they must be on a tea break. The sun is warming, and it's tiring on my eyes to read any more of the Daily Mail, so I think I'll just close them. I can hear the sea rolling against the pebbles, and the cries of the seagulls, though my hearing isn't that sharp these days. Still, the screens are keeping the breeze down, and it's very peaceful. I might just doze a while ... Just for a bit ... An afternoon nap is so welcoming.

ROGER

ST ANDREWS

Dum spiro spero
(As long as I breathe I hope)

Population: **16,000**
Unemployment: **3.5%**
Violent crimes: **13.4**
(per 1,000 per annum)
% achieving 5 or more GCSE grades A-C: **59.5**
Famous residents: **Prince William, John Knox, The Thundering Scot**

The home of Scotland's oldest university, a lovely beach, international standard golf-courses and thousands of nauseating toffs.

ALL ST. ANDREWS PHOTOS: CHRISTOPHER TRIBE

ABBEY: There used to be a rather nice abbey. It was knocked down in the sixteenth century. A few stones have been left to remind the inhabitants of what they have lost.

SEWAGE: My dad was walking down to the beach and slipped over on some marshy ground. After examining his shit-stained and reeking clothes, he soon realised that he had crossed the outlet path of a pipe discharging raw sewage into the North Sea. We had to drive home to Lancashire with the windows wound down to avoid synchronised vomiting by the whole family.

SEA SPRAY: There is a nice pier, which has two levels. A broader, lower one for the terminally cautious, and a higher, narrower one which you used to be able to walk along, blown by the sea spray and feeling as brave as Captain Birdseye. First they put a rail up to prevent people from falling in, thereby removing all the fun from the pier. Then they closed it completely. I blame the students. Or the Americans. Or Blair's nanny state. Anyhow, I know it's not my fault.

STUDENTS (I): You know the type, the Tobies and Tabithas. Pashminas and black body warmers. Fond of rugger. Parents queuing up to deposit their vile offspring three times a year in assorted Range Rovers, Audis and Saabs.

TRAINS: There is no train station. Mind you, who needs one when daddy has a fleet of Range Rovers, Audis, Saabs?

CHOPPY: I once went out on a jaunt in a pleasure boat from a town near St Andrews. The North Sea can be quite choppy and I was almost sick. Dad held firm before the vicious swell. Mum didn't. We drove home with the windows wound down.

STUDENTS (II): Having failed getting into Oxford or Cambridge, yet desperate to cling on to their bizarre public school sub-societies, they flock to

St Andrews. Worse still are those who didn't go to public school and are now desperate to get in on all the body warmer/ridiculous accents action.

DIXIE: They have a strictly all-male club called the Kate Kennedy Club or Klan. Once a year they organise a fancy-dress parade wearing pointy hats down one of St Andrews' three main streets in order to exhibit their foolishness to the whole town. Then they hold a lavish formal ball. A select number of fortunate local inhabitants receive temporary employment as waiters or bar attendants for the event.

STUDENTS (III): The problem has been compounded by the recent arrival of Prince William. So keen are the Tobies and Tabithas to catch a glimpse of our future King (all stand please), that they will voluntarily move away from the Home Counties for periods of up to thirty weeks per year. Remarkable. As an aside, I bet hard-partying Prince Hal won't be going to St Andrews; Wot! No Stringfellows?

STUDENTS (IV): So absurd is the wealth of these students and so great is the clamour to meet Wills, that rents in the town have rocketed to Kensington levels, thereby pricing out regular students – Wot! No pashminas? – and the long-suffering locals.

GOLF: St Andrews promotes itself as the Home of Golf. The town is surrounded by golf courses and its shops are rammed with golf knick-knacks and memorabilia. Golfers love golf. Americans love golf. Consequently the town is swarming with golfers, Americans and American golfers, all buzzing away in their strange leisure wear like multi-coloured flies round a golf ball-shaped shit. Lovely.
ED BAINES

....

ILL WILL
Prince William chose to study at Scotland's oldest university because he fell in love with the windswept Scottish town. Before beginning his course he said: 'I do love Scotland. There is plenty of space, I love the hills and mountains and I thought St Andrews had a real community feel to it.' However, even then he knew that: 'weekends at St Andrews ... are not particularly vibrant'. By March 2002, seven months after he started the course The Sunday Times ran a speculative report claiming that he was 'bored and lonely' in St Andrews, spending most weekends at his father's country houses, and staying in the university town for only two out of 13 weekends.
SAM JORDISON

6

LIVERPOOL
Deus Nobis Haec Otia Fecit
(God has given this unemployment unto us)

Population: 439,500
Unemployment: 6.2%
Violent crimes: 15.6
(per 1,000 per annum)
% achieving 5 or more
GCSE grades A-C: 34.7
**Famous residents: Cilla Black, Ringo
Starr, people from Brookside**

Not too long ago, Liverpool was one of
the richest, proudest cities in the world,
renowned for its native wit. Now it's the
tragically poor butt of countless bad jokes
about moustaches, tracksuits, accents and
thieving. What went wrong?

PHOTO: ART IN ACTION, BOOTLE

The tallest building in Liverpool is the 335 foot St John's Beacon, which began life as a rotating restaurant. After a fire in the nearby shopping centre, it was declared unsafe. Derelict for twenty years, it was a symbol of failure, looming over a dying city throughout the riot-torn, recession-bound Eighties. It has since been taken over by the local Radio City, and is lit up at night to match the whims of the DJs.

It has gone pink for 'Love Hour'.

It is the most stupid and useless building I have ever seen.

Coincidentally, it is situated on Williamson Square, named after the Victorian philanthropist Joseph Williamson, who retired from a successful career as a tobacco merchant to fund a series of tunnels beneath the city. He had no design, no plan, but his caves still honeycomb Edge Hill. There are chambers 70 feet long, 20 feet wide, 30 feet high. Tunnels were bricked up as soon as they were completed.

Rooms were built without doors. Men worked underground by candlelight, to no purpose.

After his wife died, Williamson threw himself into the construction of his labyrinth. He stopped going above ground, preferring the dark riddle of this improvised maze. He died in 1840, on 1 May, International Workers' Day. He was known in his time as the King of Edge Hill, and his life's work, like the beacon that now stands upon the square that bears his name, was pointless.

Such prominent monuments to uselessness are inspiring. Deranged idealism seeps into the water table of Liverpool, bubbling up in the spurts of left-wing utopianism. This socialism set it at odds with the rest of the country throughout the twentieth century. From the 1889 strike when 30,000 dockers paralysed the heart of the British empire to the 28-month strike of the dockers in 1995 (in a protest the country had to be prodded into noticing), the city acquired a reputation for rebellion, resistance, belligerence.

The refusal to fit in, that arrogance of wit and guile and talent embodied by John Lennon, is the true destiny of the Scouser, and it's just a shame that so many of us have allowed the city's character to flip between sentimentality and violence, two qualities that have long been recognised as two sides of the same coin.

Now the city is wide open, its isolated pockets of boom-time fanciness merely serving

PHOTO: JULIA HEMBER

up a decent cappuccino with which to enjoy evocative dereliction. It was during my six weeks as a security guard on Liverpool docks that I was entranced by this industrial gothic of the place, man's giant machines rusting on the harbour side, iron hulls that lie cold immensity across your thoughts. The previous eighteen years, I had merely been growing up there and consequently had never seen the city in its true light: at dawn, when the container cranes scuttle to unload freight, disturbing seagulls who arc in a stream from one sandbank to another. I think it has a potential to be a visionary city, but it still waits for its first William Blake.

MATTHEW DE ABAITUA

SPUNKA

Liverpool has more Georgian period architecture than anywhere in the UK except Bath. But unfortunately it is ruined by the graffitied sexual antics of the ubiquitous Sharon-Anne and a man called 'Spunka'.

JIMMY MACK

LORRA LORRA LOVE

A stream of professional Scousers that never return home remind us how great it is while actually reinforcing how bad it is. Like Cilla Black – harking on about how much she loves the place from the benign safety of her Berkshire home.

How do you deserve another chance when ambassadors like these are being let loose on the rest of us? Liverpool coats itself in this sugary miasma, as if everyone from outside the place has collective amnesia to the filth and grime of the place and the sordid, petty nature of its inhabitants.

TOM BRAIDER

WINCHESTER*

Population: **107,222**
Unemployment: **1.4%**
Violent crimes: **6.8 (per 1,000 per annum)**
% achieving 5+ GCSE grades A-C: **82**
Famous residents: **David Gower, Izaac Walton (revered author of The Compleat Angler), Jane Austen**

A town that owes its continuing prosperity to the presence of one of the world's poshest schools in its centre. Winchester's undoubted beauty is scarred by the broken-beer bottle violence of its Friday nights and its mellow flavour soured by the priggish complacency of its inhabitants.

* The town has no motto. Its set of arms comes from the days before people started using them. Typical.

ALL WINCHESTER PHOTOS: KEVIN PARR

Sure it's pretty and historic, but it's hardly the bastion of civility many would have you believe.

Any character disappeared from the town centre when the high street received the chain store makeover; house prices are exorbitant and cater exclusively for well-heeled London-employed family-builders seeking old England. The countryside has been hewn by Maggie Thatcher's M3 legacy. And that isn't the half of it. It's the middle-class complacency, nay arro-

"CHARACTER DISAPPEARED...
WHEN THE HIGH STREET RECEIVED
THE CHAIN-STORE MAKEOVER"

gance that defines the place.

This reactionary character is personified by the town's most odious institution, Winchester College, and its inmates. Young public school boys stride the historic streets, comfortable and sublimely superior in the knowledge that daddy's considerable land-ownership and board-room interests will see them through to their positions as Tory MPs and beyond.

JOHN MITCHELL

....

FIGHT NIGHTS

I started going out in Winchester in the very late Eighties, and the nightlife defined nondescript. Half-hearted wine bars, tired pubs and yet a lovely air of security. Doors were held open, girls sat gorgeous with red wine and Marlboro lights, and no-one barged at the bar.

There used to be a fair bit of mouth, admittedly, but back then fights were avoided. What grief did occur was invariably instigated by the squaddies. On night release from the bar-racks, they reeled into town, all wolf-whistles and rolling shoulders. Yet they were easily avoid-ed, and stuck to their own predetermined terri-tories, only passing out swift justice to the fools so foolish, or drunk, that they felt invincible to a war machine. But with the barracks sold, and the soldiers gone, Winchester fragmented. With no military police at the top of the pecking order, splinter groups emerged. Armed with acne, Eminem, and puffa jackets, the crew (sorry, kru)

had arrived.

Their aims – never venture out in a gang less then twenty strong; spit at all times; if white then walk and talk like the American urban gangsters whose records you buy; force old ladies to step off the pavement; and, of course, initialise aggrava-tion with any individual or group whom you outnumber by at least four to one.

I was unfortunate enough to run into a gang one night. They were at least twelve strong, had already assaulted my girlfriend, and sexually assaulted one of her friends, so I was fair game. They cornered me behind parked cars, glassed me, and then pum-melled me enough to miss a week's work through concussion. Of course the police were called, and to be fair they were prompt and concerned. Yes they even knew who was responsible, but all they could do was arrest and caution with common assault, thus leaving me as a named and identifiable future victim rather than just a random punchbag on a street corner.

Perhaps I should have learned from my friend Mike, who one evening brought his toy water pistol into town – a worryingly realistic replica handgun. At the end of the night, trouble, as usual, was kicking off near the taxi queue. Two of my friends were accosted by 15 mouthy fifteen-year-olds, and then a car load of their equally irritating older brothers.

Mike, meanwhile, across the road, had had enough and just wanted to get home. And so, with his hair swept back and his long coat flailing, he marched toward the melee, pulling his gun. In his thick Irish drawl shouted, 'Just who the fuck do you think you're messing with, pal?' Exit everyone, but us, and a very cooperative taxi-driver.

ANON.

CRAP TOWN TRIVIA *Winchester has one of the world's finest collections of fifteenth-century graffiti scattered around the cloisters of Winchester College.*

IN DEFENCE OF WINCHESTER

It is always reassuring to find the exception that proves the rule. Four million visitors a year come to Winchester, and the regular interviews we carry out suggest that they love it and that they return time and again. In a recent comparison with other towns and cities in England, Winchester outstripped all other destinations when scored by more than 500 visitors for 'general atmosphere' and 'feeling of welcome', 'feeling of safety' and 'overall enjoyment of visit'. The city also led the field in terms of the quality of its shopping environment and the quality of service offered.

A very small number of interviewees felt that their visit could indeed have been better – if it had not been raining, or if the queue at the pizza restaurant had been shorter or, indeed, if their girlfriends had not spent so much time shopping. But the great majority relished their time here, specifically mentioning the welcoming people, the culture and the tranquillity of the city.

As a democratic nation, we tend to go with a majority vote. Ninety-four per cent of our visitors say they would recommend Winchester to others. But for every Labour landslide, there are a few votes cast to the Monster Raving Loony party. We suggest that the best way to decide is a visit.

ELOISE APPLEBY
HEAD OF TOURISM FOR WINCHESTER CITY COUNCIL

HYTHE
Hythe's alive!

4

Population: **16,000**
Unemployment: **2%**
Violent crimes: **9.1**
(per 1,000 per annum)
% achieving 5+ GCSE
grades A-C: **26**
Famous residents: **Michael
Howard MP**

A small, pretty place on the south
coast that gives real purpose to the
nearby cliffs, Hythe has a maritime
record dating back to the 1st
century AD when the Romans used
it as one of the landing posts for
their invasion force. However,
Hythe's history appears to have
ended in 1918. Nothing noteworthy
has happened there since. In fact,
very little has happened at all.

ALL HYTHE PHOTOS: SAM JORDISON

You don't have to be a regular contributor to the 'Straight To The Point' section of the Daily Mail Letters page to live in Hythe. Neither is it essential, if you want to rise to a position of authority, say a greengrocer or co-ordinator of a Neighbourhood Watch scheme, to have a mild yet unfortunate facial disfigurement. But boy does it help. Perhaps the most spirit-crushingly tedious town in Kent (quite a plaudit), Hythe is the place that makes nearby Folkestone look like Las Vegas.

So utterly bereft are Hythe folk of anything resembling spirit that they are incapable of even the more admirable of suburban excesses like backbiting gossip or wife-swapping. Instead, there are just swathes of old men and women patrolling the streets, bored out of their wits.

This is the sort of town where a cup of tea and a scone in a local cafe is considered not so much a treat but an act of outrageous decadence. The sort of town where Ian Duncan-Smith is regarded as rather too liberal. The sort of town where incest rules to such an extent that men give themselves Father's Day cards.

Visit the town's post office, and you'll find racks of postcards featuring images of Hythe's sun-kissed beach full of happy families and other images of small town serenity. But turn around on your way out, and you'll see the real heart of Hythe. A gaggle of bored, mute twelve-year-old boys dressed in 1980s style shellsuits, sitting dejected on a bench outside the High Street's Iceland store, with only an adolescence of cider, incest and Airfix models to look forward to.

CHAS NEWKEY-BURDEN

POSTSCRIPT
This piece on Hythe was originally published on The Idler website. A few weeks afterwards I received an email from a man who worked promoting Hythe as a tourist destination. Expecting to find inside the wrath of the provinces, I opened the email with some trepidation.

'Not sure about the incest', he wrote, 'but the rest is spot on.' My correspondent has since left his job in Hythe, but I remain indebted to him for such positive and moving literary criticism.

....

IN DEFENCE OF HYTHE
I suppose beauty is in the eye of the beholder and Chas Newkey-Burden's standards can best be assessed by his self-confessed admiration of backbiting gossip and wifeswapping. Measured by those standards Hythe may indeed be found wanting.

But for those with different standards – the vast majority of people – Hythe is the jewel of Kent. It is an immensely attractive town, which attracts visitors from far and wide. I suggest that if any of your readers would like to make a comparative assessment of the various judgements that have been made about its attractions they come and see for themselves!

MICHAEL HOWARD;
FORMER HOME-SECRETARY AND CURRENT MP FOR FOLKESTONE AND HYTHE

MORECAMBE
Beauty surrounds, health abounds

Population: **45,000**
Unemployment: **4.2%**
Violent crimes: **9.2 (per
1,000 per annum)**
% achieving 5 or more
GCSE grades A-C: **47**
(Morecambe High School)
Famous residents: **The Great
Suprendo, Eric Morecambe, the
late Dame Thora Hird**

A Northwestern seaside resort that has
until recently promoted itself as a small
version of Blackpool. It offers a
spectacular view over its sandy bay to the
stately southern fells of the Lake District.
After a brief heyday in the 1930s the town
has suffered a long, sad decline.

ALL MORECAMBE PHOTOS: SAM JORDISON

Poor old Morecambe. The seaside town they should never have opened. Where a silent and grey day comes as a blessed relief from the gales of black depression that generally batter its desolate promenades.

I can't possibly think why anyone would ever go to Morecambe, unless of course they're unlucky enough to live there, or are attracted to misery and squalor in the same way hearty moor-walking Victorians used to be attracted to graveyards and consumption.

It long ago seems to have forgotten about being a holiday resort. Its attractions hunch empty and unused on the seafront.

The town would be almost entirely empty if it wasn't for the fact that the DHSS have put its Bed & Breakfasts to good use in housing the Northwest's homeless and hopelessly addicted. You are now more likely to find needles on the prom than lollipop sticks, and the cheery face of naughty holiday sex that Morecambe once tried to show to the world has been covered in lesions.

SAM JORDISON

HOW I DEARLY WISH
I WAS NOT HERE

BIRD, SHIT

BAD COUNCIL

In 1993 Morecambe became the site of one of Noel Edmunds' ill fated 'Crinkly Bottom' projects, cashing in on the popularity of Mr Blobby. The park that was built was closed almost as soon as it opened. The eventual settlement with Noel Edmunds' Unique Group cost the local council over £2 million (including legal fees), costs that council tax payers in the deprived borough are still paying. A district auditor brought in to clear up the fallout described the theme park scheme as 'disastrous'. He said that the Council's actions had been 'irrational' 'imprudent', 'unlawful', and 'mistaken'.

IN DEFENCE OF MORECAMBE

When I first took the job here twelve years ago people said to me: 'Why on earth are you going to Morecambe? It's a dive,' and they weren't far wrong – but I believed then and I believe now it does have a lot going for it. The Eighties and early Nineties were especially bad, with stuff closing and low visitor numbers, but it's picked up since then with £50 million being spent in the last decade and corresponding increases in visitors. Much of the central area has been redeveloped with new bowling alleys, a cinema and a successful theatre, which has recently hosted the RSC. We've demolished three blocks of dilapidated buildings and replaced them with parks, and a multi-million pound redevelopment of the beautiful art-deco Midland hotel into a five-star establishment is underway. It will take another two or three years until the regeneration work is complete, but we have recognised that markets have changed and we are now changing with them.

JIM TROTMAN, PRINCIPLE TOURIST OFFICER

THE UK'S FIRST ART DECO HOTEL HAS BEEN ROTTING FOR DECADES, WAITING FOR 'PENDING' REDEVLOPMENT

MORECAMBE AMENITIES
Bubbles Leisure Complex (closed)
Frontierland Western Theme Park (closed) **Blobbyland** (closed)
The Midland Hotel (closed)

145

CUMBERNAULD
Spe Expectamus (We wait in hope)

Population: 48,000
Unemployment: 5.5%
Violent crimes: 19 (per 1,000 per annum)
% gaining 5 awards at level 3 or above: 96
Famous residents: **Ken Buchanan (boxer)**

Cumbernauld lies in the centre of Scotland and is famous for being the setting for Gregory's Girl. So bad is the design of its centre - a platform raised on stilts over a network of tunnels and bunkers - that town-planning students visit the town as an example of what not to do.

PHOTO: SAM JORDISON

147

It is a run-down new town with the fun of 1960s concrete innovation and the joy of Thatcherite neglect – and getting worse. It is grey, grim, redundant, aggressive and soulless. It boasts a half-demolished centre (which has been that way for three years). The police regularly hunt young people from the streets into the tunnels of its bizarre architecture. There are no leisure facilities

CRAP TOWN TRIVIA

AWARD WINNINGLY BAD

In 2001 Cumbernauld town centre scooped the 'Plook On The Plinth' award for being the most dismal place in Scotland, in the Carbuncle Awards for bad architecture. Judges described the town centre as 'a rabbit warren on stilts' and 'a structure that would not look out of place in Kabul'. Two months later, the BBC gave the town another award for having the worst house in Britain.

apart from lawn bowls and a swimming pool. There are only two clubs, both of which regularly host bottle-tossing contests. There are streets and areas that are so dangerous and dilapidated that badgers won't go near them.

GARY HAYES

INNOCENCE LOST

I was a Cumbernauld resident for most of my young life. I was growing up in the town when it was looking promising and was a place full of potential adventures, but maybe that was just because I was a kid.

I remember when there were rumours that a Marks & Spencer store was going to open ... it was as if the Messiah had returned. This, of course, was all bollocks and people were once again disappointed. Then the new Asda opened and I even found myself going to Asda at times because there was nothing else to do. You know it's bad when Asda becomes a local night spot.

It seems a long time ago when Gregory's Girl was filmed and they lay on the grass in the last scene and danced away laughing. Such innocent times! If that happened today Gregory's face would have been ripped open with a broken bottle from ear to ear by a gang of neds who drink in the park. Claire Grogan would be screaming in fear, getting molested while Gregory walks around dazed, as blood pisses from his face.

VINNIE BROWNLOW

BAD COUNCIL

A large amount of the blame for Cumbernauld's current dilapidated state has been laid at the feet of North Lanarkshire Council and its predecessors. Gordon Young for instance, the Carbuncle Chairman, accused North Lanarkshire Council of seriously neglecting the town.

In its defence, the council has since stated that they are in the process of investing in and redeveloping the town centre, and that improvements will soon be seen. However, Brian Yule from the Cumbernauld News says that redevelopment 'should have been completed in 1997, then 1999, then 2001'.

'However,' he added, 'every time it seems that progress is being made, the developers are fired.'

HULL
The gateway to Europe

Population: **243,595**
Unemployment: **6%**
Violent crime: **15.3 (per 1,000 per annum)**
% achieving 5+ GCSE grades A-C: **28.9 (The lowest percentage in the country)**
Famous residents: **Philip Larkin, Paul Heaton, John Prescott**

The city of Hull, isolated from the rest of the country by the Humber estuary, has had more than its fair share of social deprivation and tragedy. It suffered terribly during World War II and a large proportion of its traditional industries have since collapsed. Unemployment rates are high, as are crime and heroin addiction levels. It is, however, increasingly successful, with a busy shopping and cultural centre and it contains a large, thriving student population.

HULL - IT SMELLS OF DEATH

How can I describe Hull? Take a prosperous town, a gem of the Northeast, with a rich maritime industry. Sprinkle it generously with Luftwaffe bombs for a few years until its heart is a gutted shell. Kill off its seagoing heritage and plunge its young men and women into generations of soul-destroying unemployment. Then let a bunch of lunatic architects loose in the Sixties and Seventies and apply gallons of concrete.

The silent threat of violence hangs in the air, along with the smell from the chocolate factory. Chocolate factories, by the way, don't smell of chocolate, they smell of death. If the wind comes from the southeast the smell of Grimsby docks adds a fishy staleness to the odour. If it comes from the other direction it brings the smell of the tanning factory … rotting carcasses and rancid flesh.

Hull did teach me one valuable lesson. No matter what happens to me in later life, no matter where I live, or how bad things are, I will know that it can never, ever be as bad as living in Hull.

I must insist that I have nothing against the inhabitants, just the town itself. I'm sure that on Judgement Day the good people of Hull will be first through the Pearly Gates. I fear however that Hull itself will be leased out indefinitely to Satan to provide ample housing for the Damned.
FINLAY COUTTS-BRITON

PASTORAL HULL

I agree that some of the architecture leaves a lot to be desired. But what has to be remembered is that the place was bombed heavily in WWII and we never had the same clout as London, so while they had the cash to rebuild

BAD COUNCIL

As recently as 1999, Hull was said to be the richest local authority in Britain after the sale of their share in the local telephone exchange, Kingston Communications, netted them £263m. They blew the lot, and more, within three years, embarking on a £650million spending spree. £40million was spent building a football stadium for the failing Hull City Football Club. A year later, the club called in administrators after the players had not been paid for five weeks. The streets were cleaned and re-graffitied just as quickly. A fortune was spent on central heating and double

CRAP TOWN TRIVIA *The poet Philip Larkin spent most of his days as a resident of Hull. He famously said: "I wish I could think of just one nice thing I could tell you about Hull, oh yes... it's very nice and flat for cycling."*

There are no hills in Hull. This has convinced even the night to abandon the town. Combined with close proximity to the sea, near constant low-level cloud cover after dark, and high levels of light pollution, the flatness causes the sky to glow orange once the sun has set.

properly, we had to make do with second best.

That said, there are many gems, such as the cobbled High Street, the home of anti-slavery pioneer William Wilberforce, and Holy Trinity Church, the largest brick parish church in England.

There's a quality of life that most people in London can only dream of. Consider this, my southern chums in your 250 grand one-bedroom 'city apartments'. I bought last year, a three-bed semi in a quiet suburb of Hull overlooking open fields, with a double garage and workshop, a sauna, conservatory and front and rear gardens, for 70k.

Go to a place where you can

glazing in empty council houses. Many of these houses are now scheduled for demolition. £32million was spent covering a "funding gap" in day-to-day spending.

By 2003 the estimated annual overspend for Hull City Council was £8.4million: £2.5million more than they "expected".

Chris Jarvis, an independent Hull council veter-

an says that the council have been "behaving like children in a sweet shop." The people of one of the poorest regions in the country are now paying for this profligacy with ever increasing council tax bills.

talk to real people who won't judge you by your job, wealth or title. Go into a strange pub and chat to the bloke next to you and discover that his uncle and your dad were mates on the trawlers. Then see if the shape of a building matters more to you than human warmth. Added to this is boundless solitude. In literally ten minutes, I can either be on top of a deserted hill in the Yorkshire Wolds, or gazing at the setting sun on the shores of the Humber river, with no one around in sight – and that's something money can't buy.

SIMON MASON

IT'S GOOD TO TALK

Hull, along with Liverpool, is one of the friendliest places I've lived

Hull does have the most imaginative street name – The Land Of Green Ginger.

PHIL HEARNE

in. People talk to each other, yes really, strangers and everything. And it has more liberal licensing laws than London.

We are also the only place in Britain to be out-side of the BT hegemony, our phone network is more modern than BT's and a damn sight cheaper, 6p for an unlimited length local call at all times.

DOMINIC FORBES

PHONE BOOTH HORROR

The only time I was in Hull, I went into a phone booth and found that someone had crapped on the floor. The calls may be cheap, but it's a high price to pay for having to share a phone box with a (human) turd.

ALISON LANE

HULL HAEMORRAGING PEOPLE

In 1999 there were more than 10,000 empty homes in Hull, almost half of them council properties. Between 1999 and January 2003 2,121 were destroyed. Chris Jarvis, a cabinet member for housing on Hull city council, says: "We have fine, well-built council property which, if it was in any other northern city - and definitely in the south - would be well sought after."

THE HUNT GOES ON

We're going to dig deeper into the crap that covers the UK. For 40 days and 40 nights Crap Towns editors Sam Jordison and Dan Kieran will be travelling around the British wilderness visiting as many towns as possible to judge just how bad they are.

If you would like to nominate a town for us to visit, email theidlers@idler.co.uk and tell us why you think it's so awful. The writer of our favourite entry will win one year's subscription to The Idler magazine.

If you see a car with a big snail on it, and two scruffy looking young men wandering round your town carrying clipboards and pretending to be posh to test local aggression levels, the chances are that you've come across us. The first person to correctly identify us, and buy us a drink, will win an idler T-shirt.

The results of the quest will be published in 2004.